High Romantic Argument

M. H. ABRAMS

High Romantic Argument
ESSAYS FOR M. H. ABRAMS

ESSAYS BY

GEOFFREY HARTMAN   THOMAS MCFARLAND

JONATHAN WORDSWORTH   LAWRENCE LIPKING

WAYNE C. BOOTH   JONATHAN CULLER

WITH A REPLY BY M. H. ABRAMS

A PREFACE BY STEPHEN M. PARRISH

AND A BIBLIOGRAPHY BY STUART A. ENDE

EDITED BY

LAWRENCE LIPKING

CORNELL UNIVERSITY PRESS

ITHACA AND LONDON

First published 1981 by Cornell University Press.
Published in the United Kingdom by Cornell University Press Ltd.,
Ely House, 37 Dover Street, London W1X 4HQ.

International Standard Book Number 0-8014-1307-9
Library of Congress Catalog Card Number 80-69830
Printed in the United States of America
*Librarians: Library of Congress cataloging information appears
on the last page of the book*

Contents

[5]

Preface

The papers in this volume were delivered at a two-day symposium sponsored by the Society for the Humanities at Cornell University in April 1978. Not without honor in his own house, M. H. Abrams had been more formally honored elsewhere (as we his colleagues were aware)—in Charlottesville and Chicago, Texas and Toronto, Bloomington and Boston, not to speak of Trumpington and Iffley. With the modest aim of reminding him of our own high local esteem, we resolved to bring to Ithaca from some of those distant places a group of his friends and peers to celebrate his presence among us.

The papers presented by these friends and peers reveal brilliantly what Abrams' larger presence—his presence in the profession—has meant. The papers were arranged so as to touch the major kinds of Abrams' achievement—his studies in Wordsworth and Coleridge, his contribution to the history of ideas, his work in critical theory. A fourth kind of achievement, touched only lightly, deserves special mention, and that is his contribution to the teaching of English in America. Here the incomparable *Norton Anthology of English Literature,* which (through four editions) has informed a whole generation of undergraduate students, stands as testimony to Abrams' skill and sensitivity as an interpreter of literature. Like all his other works, and like his teaching, the anthology is marked throughout by distinctive virtues rarely found in combination: it is subtle, literate, and deeply learned, yet free of pedantry and always intelligible to the serious reader. These virtues are not confined to M. H. Abrams' professional work, as anyone who knows him, or has spent any time at Cornell in the past thirty years, will understand: they mark the man, as well. At once benevolent and stimulating as a colleague, unfailingly humane in his attitudes, he has helped to teach us how to live—how to share his own robust enjoyment in the life of the mind and of the spirit. His special balance of grace and power, of civil urbanity and analytical rigor, can be sensed in the *ex tempore* response that closes this volume (taken from a tape recording and very lightly edited). There as eloquently as anywhere else are revealed the distinctive virtues that we have come to cherish and that we here desire to honor.

STEPHEN M. PARRISH

Ithaca, New York

Editor's Note

This book has a plot. Like any collection of essays by various hands, to be sure, it goes off in many directions. The critics and historians who have contributed to it do not necessarily agree with one another, or even with the critic and historian they celebrate. Yet they do share a common problem; and together their efforts to solve it fall into a pattern.

The problem, easier to state than to manage, is simply what to make of the work of M. H. Abrams. I do not mean by this only that Abrams provides the subject and occasion of these essays, but also that something in his achievement—perhaps its very solidity—puzzles a good many modern readers. Many of these contributors regard Abrams' work as more problematic than he does himself. In an age when the writing of history is often equated with the writing of fiction, when every statement of fact is scrutinized for the metaphors that inform it, his accomplishment seems to belong to another, more coherent world. He believes in history, evidence, reason, meaning, authors, texts, himself; he remains an unreconstructed humanist. Such clarity of purpose can be troubling. Hence several of these essays establish a relationship to Abrams' books by darkening their counsel, reading in them, as Keats in the face of night, "huge cloudy symbols of a high romance."

Collectively, indeed, the plot of this book might be viewed as a version of Ovid's *Metamorphoses,* translating the living being of Abrams into a series of transcendent metaphors or constellations. The process is clearest in Wayne Booth's galaxy of metaphors, but it occurs elsewhere as well. Thus Geoffrey Hartman and Jonathan Wordsworth depart from William Wordsworth's express "program for poetry," as formulated in *Natural Supernaturalism,* to draw attention to other aspects of the poet, moving from the spheres of time and speech to prophecy and silence. Thomas McFarland canonizes Abrams' books into twin monuments; my own essay rearranges them into images and motives of literary history; and Jonathan Culler deconstructs them to paradoxes of language. In some respects, perhaps, the process of metamorphosis may go too far. There is relatively little discussion here, for example, of the specific views of romantic poetry and thought that many readers associate with Abrams' name. Often these essays seem shy of the books, or view them at the respectful distance of a telescope. Yet that shyness, related to awe, may also indicate the continuing power of *The Mirror and the Lamp* and *Natural Supernaturalism* to sway us from afar. They cannot be safely relegated to some nebulous afterlife; they remain alive right here and now.

Nor is it merely by courtesy, in this volume, that the last word should be given to Abrams himself. The plot requires it. Through all the different points of view this book expresses, through all its metamorphoses, one element of suspense keeps recurring: how well can Abrams' work sustain its own integrity when so much has been made of it? "Woe unto me when all men praise me!" There is always the danger that such rituals of praising will lapse into empty ceremony. But that does not happen here. Abrams' response deftly points out the issue behind the ceremony: whether his work is to be absorbed into metaphor or debated and argued. With friendly firmness he refuses to lie down in someone else's plot, and insists on being taken seriously as a humanist and scholar. It is a harmonious ending—but not *too* harmonious. For the plot of this book does not consist, in the end, of a canonization so much as a debate without conclusion; individual human voices joined in mental fight. The discussion comes down to earth; the subject strikes back. And what we are left with in this book, finally, is not the cloudy symbols of a high romance but a genuine high romantic argument.

LAWRENCE LIPKING

Evanston, Illinois

PART I
VISIONS OF
WORDSWORTH

The Poetics of Prophecy

GEOFFREY HARTMAN

1

In our honorific or sophomoric moods, we like to think that
poets are prophets. At least that certain great poets have something of the audacity and intensity—the strong speech—of Old
Testament prophets who claimed that the word of God came to
them. "The words of Jeremiah, the son of Hilkiah . . . To whom
the word of the Lord came in the days of Josiah . . ." It is hard to
understand even this introductory passage, for the word for
"words," *divre* in Hebrew, indicates something closer to "acts" or
"word events," while what the King James version translates as
"to whom the word of the Lord came," which hypostatizes the
Word, as if it had a being of its own, or were consubstantial with
what we know of God, is in the original simply *hajah devar-adonai
elav*, "the God-word was to him." We don't know, in short, what
is going on; yet through a long tradition of translation and interpretation we feel we know. Similarly, when Wordsworth tells
us that around his twenty-third year he "received" certain "con-
victions," which included the thought that despite his humbler
subject matter he could stand beside the "men of old," we seek
gropingly to make sense of that conviction. "Poets, even as
Prophets," Wordsworth writes,

[15]

each with each
Connected in a mighty scheme of truth,
Have each his own peculiar faculty,
Heaven's gift, a sense that fits him to perceive
Objects unseen before . . .
An insight that in some sort he possesses,
A privilege whereby a work of his,
Proceeding from a source of untaught things
Creative and enduring, may become
A power like one of Nature's.

[1850 *Prelude* xiii.301-12]

In the earlier (1805) version of *The Prelude* "insight" is "influx," which relates more closely to a belief in inspiration, or a flow (of words) the poet participates in yet does not control: "An influx, that in some sort I possess'd."

I will somewhat neglect in what follows one difference, rather obvious, between poet and prophet. A prophet is to us, and perhaps to himself, mainly a *voice*—as God himself seems to him primarily a voice. Even when he does God in many voices, they are not felt to stand in an equivocal relation to each other: each voice is absolute, and vacillation produces vibrancy rather than ambiguity. In this sense there is no "poetics of prophecy"; there is simply a voice breaking forth, a quasivolcanic eruption, and sometimes its opposite, the "still, small voice" heard after the thunder of Sinai. I will try to come to grips with that difference between poet and prophet later on; here I should only note that, being of the era of Wordsworth rather than of Jeremiah, I must look back from the poet's rather than from the prophet's perspective, while acknowledging that the very concept of poetry may be used by Wordsworth to reflect on—and often to defer—the claim that he has a prophetic gift.

There is another passage in *The Prelude* that explores the relation between poet and prophet. Wordsworth had been to France during the Revolution, had followed that cataclysmic movement in hope, had seen it degenerate into internecine politics and aggressive war. Yet despite the discrediting of revolutionary ideals, something of his faith survived, and not only faith but, as he strangely put it, "daring sympathies with power." In brief, he saw those terrible events in France as necessary and even divinely sanctioned. To explain his mood Wordsworth writes a confessional passage that also gives his most exact understanding of prophecy:

> But as the ancient Prophets, borne aloft
> In vision, yet constrained by natural laws
> With them to take a troubled human heart,
> Wanted not consolations, nor a creed
> Of reconcilement, then when they denounced,
> On towns and cities, wallowing in the abyss
> Of their offences, punishment to come;
> Or saw, like other men, with bodily eyes,
> Before them, in some desolated place,
> The wrath consummate and the threat fulfilled;
> So, with devout humility be it said,
> So, did a portion of that spirit fall
> On me uplifted from the vantage-ground
> Of pity and sorrow to a state of being
> That through the time's exceeding fierceness saw
> Glimpses of retribution, terrible,
> And in the order of sublime behests:
> But, even if that were not, amid the awe
> Of unintelligible chastisement,
> Not only acquiescences of faith
> Survived, but daring sympathies with power,
> Motions not treacherous or profane, else why
> Within the folds of no ungentle breast
> Their dread vibration to this hour prolonged?
> Wild blasts of music thus could find their way
> Into the midst of turbulent events;
> So that worst tempests might be listened to.
> [1850 *Prelude* x.437–63]

This eloquent statement has many complexities; but it is clear that though Wordsworth felt himself "uplifted from the vantage-ground / Of pity and sorrow," he did not leave them behind in this moment of sublime vision and terrible purification. It is certainly a remarkable feature of a prophet like Jeremiah that "borne aloft / In vision" he yet takes with him "a troubled human heart." Like Jonah, he tries to evade the commission, though not, like Jonah, by running away but rather by claiming he is not of age when it comes to speech ("Then said I, Ah, Lord GOD! behold, I cannot speak: for I am a child"). Jeremiah even accuses God, in bitterness of heart, of the very thing of which God accused Israel: of seducing the prophet, or of being unfaithful (Jeremiah 20:7ff).

Wordsworth expresses most strongly a further, related aspect of prophetical psychology: the ambivalent sympathy shown by the prophet for the powerful and terrible thing he envisions. This sympathy operates even when he tries to avert what must be, or to find a "creed of reconcilement." The poet's problem vis-à-vis the Revolution was not, principally, that he had to come to terms with crimes committed in the name of the Revolution or of liberty. For at the end of the passage from which I have quoted he indicates that there had been a rebound of faith, a persuasion that grew in him that the Revolution itself was not to blame, but rather "a terrific reservoir of guilt / And ignorance filled up from age to age" had "burst and spread in deluge through the land." The real problem was his entanglement in a certain order of sensations which endured to the very time of writing: he owns to "daring sympathies with power," "motions," whose "dread vibration" is "to this hour prolonged," and whose harmonizing effect in the midst of the turbulence he characterized by the oxymoron "Wild blasts of music."

We understand perfectly well that what is involved in Wordsworth's sympathy with power is not, or not simply, a sublime kind of *Schadenfreude*. And that no amount of talk about the pleasure given by tragedy, through "cathartic" identification, would do more than uncover the same problem in a related area. The seduction power exerts, when seen as an act of God or

Nature, lies within common experience. It does not of itself distinguish poets or prophets. What is out of the ordinary here is the "dread vibration": a term close to music, as well as one that conveys the lasting resonance of earlier feelings. How did Wordsworth's experience of sympathy with power accrue a metaphor made overt in "wild blasts of music"?

The tradition that depicts inspired poetry as a wild sort of natural music ("Homer the great Thunderer, [and] the voice that roars along the bed of Jewish Song") circumscribes rather than explains these metaphors. When we take them to be more than commonplaces of high poetry we notice that they sometimes evoke the force of wind and water as blended sound (cf. "The stationary blasts of waterfalls," 1850 *Prelude* vi.626), a sound with power to draw the psyche in, as if the psyche also were an instrument or element, and had to mingle responsively with some overwhelming, massive unity. Despite the poet's imagery of violence, the ideal of harmony, at least on the level of sound, is not given up. The soul as a gigantic if reluctant aeolian harp is implicitly evoked.

How strangely this impulse to harmony is linked with violent feelings can be shown by one of Wordsworth's similes. Similes are, of course, a formal way of bringing together, or harmonizing, different areas of experience. From Coleridge to the New Critics the discussion of formal poetics has often focused on the valorized distinction between fancy and imagination, or on the way difference is reconciled. Shortly before his reflection on the ancient prophets, and when he is still describing the indiscriminate carnage unleashed by Robespierre, Wordsworth has recourse to a strange pseudo-Homeric simile comparing the tempo of killings to a child activating a toy windmill:

> though the air
> Do of itself blow fresh, and make the vanes
> Spin in his eyesight, *that* contents him not,
> But, with the plaything at arm's length, he sets

His front against the blast, and runs amain,
That it may whirl the faster.

[1850 *Prelude* x.369-74]

An aeolian toy is used, explicitly now, to image a sublime and terrible order of events. The instrument is given to the wind, so that it may go faster; yet this childish sport is set in an ominous context. The innocent wish to have something go fast reflects on the child whose mimicry (as in the Intimations Ode) suggests his haste to enter the very world where that haste has just shown itself in heinous form. Though there is something incongruous in the simile, there is also something fitting: or at least a drive toward fitting together incongruous passions of childhood and adulthood; and may this drive not express the dark "workmanship that reconciles / Discordant elements" by a mysterious, quasi-musical "harmony" (1850 *Prelude* i.340ff.)? Here the reconciling music, by which the mind is built up, is already something of a "wild blast"; and when we think of the passage on prophecy to follow, on Wordsworth's "daring sympathies with power," we realize that what is involved in these various instances—lust for carnage, vertigo-sport, the child's impatience to grow up, the poet's fit of words, and the prophet's sympathy with the foreseen event, however terrible—is an anticipatory relation to time, a hastening of futurity.

The music metaphor, associated with wind and water sound, occurs in yet another context close to apocalyptic feelings. (By "apocalyptic" I always mean quite specifically an anticipatory, proleptic relation to time, intensified to the point where there is at once desire for and dread of the end being hastened. There is a potential inner turning against time, and against nature insofar as it participates in the temporal order.) Wordsworth's dream in *Prelude* v of the Arab saving stone and shell from the encroaching flood, also identified as the two principal branches of humane learning, mathematics and literature, is given an explicitly apocalyptic frame. The poet is meditating on books "that aspire to an unconquerable life," human creations that must perish nevertheless. Quoting from a Shakespeare sonnet on the theme of time, he reflects that we "weep to have" what we may lose: the weeping represents both the vain effort and the proleptic regret, so that the very joy of possessing lies close to tears, or thoughts deeper than tears. Only one detail of the ensuing dream need concern us. It comes when the Arab asks the dreamer to hold the shell (poetry) to his ear. "I did so," says the dreamer,

> And heard that instant in an unknown tongue,
> Which yet I understood, articulate sounds,
> A loud prophetic blast of harmony;
> An Ode, in passion uttered, which foretold
> Destruction to the children of the earth
> By deluge, now at hand.
> [1850 *Prelude* v.93–98]

A "blast of harmony" is not only a more paradoxical, more acute version of the metaphor in "blast of music," but we recognize it as an appropriate figure for the shouting poetry also called prophecy. In the lines that follow, Wordsworth stresses the dual function of such poetry: it has power to exhilarate and to soothe the human heart. But this is a gloss that conventionalizes the paradox in "blast of harmony" and does not touch the reality of the figure.

Our task is to understand the reality of figures, or more precisely, the reality of "blast of harmony," when applied to prophecy, or prophetic poetry. I will suggest, on the basis of this figure, that there is a poetics of prophecy; and I will study it by reading closely two episodes in *The Prelude* entirely within the secular sphere: the "spot of time" alluding to the death of the poet's father, and the ascent of Snowdon. After that a transition to the prophetic books, and to Jeremiah in particular, may lie open.

2

The death of Wordsworth's father is not attended by unusual circumstances. As Claudius says in a play we shall refer to again: a "common theme / Is death of fathers." Yet it is precisely the commonplace that releases in this case the "dread vibration." The thirteen-year-old schoolboy is impatient to return home for the Christmas holidays, and climbs a crag overlooking two highways to see whether he can spot the horses that should be coming. From that bare, wind-blown crag he watches intensely, and shortly after he returns home his father dies. That is all: a moment of intense, impatient watching, and then, ten days later, the death. Two things without connection except contiguity in time come together in the boy, who feels an emotion that perpetuates "down to this very time" the sights and sounds he experienced waiting for the horses. Here is Wordsworth's account in full:

> There rose a crag,
> That, from the meeting-point of two highways
> Ascending, overlooked them both, far stretched;
> Thither, uncertain on which road to fix
> My expectation, thither I repaired,
> Scout-like, and gained the summit; 'twas a day
> Tempestuous, dark, and wild, and on the grass
> I sate half-sheltered by a naked wall;
> Upon my right hand couched a single sheep,
> Upon my left a blasted hawthorn stood;
> With those companions at my side, I watched,
> Straining my eyes intensely, as the mist
> Gave intermitting prospect of the copse
> And plain beneath. Ere we to school returned,—
> That dreary time,—ere we had been ten days
> Sojourners in my father's house, he died,
> And I and my three brothers, orphans then,
> Followed his body to the grave. The event,
> With all the sorrow that it brought, appeared
> A chastisement; and when I called to mind
> That day so lately past, when from the crag

I looked in such anxiety of hope;
With trite reflections of morality,
Yet in the deepest passion, I bowed low
To God, Who thus corrected my desires;
And, afterwards, the wind and sleety rain,
And all the business of the elements,
The single sheep, and the one blasted tree,
And the bleak music from that old stone wall,
The noise of wood and water, and the mist
That on the line of each of those two roads
Advanced in such indisputable shapes;
All these were kindred spectacles and sounds
To which I oft repaired, and thence would drink,
As at a fountain; and on winter nights,
Down to this very time, when storm and rain
Beat on my roof, or, haply, at noon-day,
While in a grove I walk, whose lofty trees,
Laden with summer's thickest foliage, rock
In a strong wind, some working of the spirit,
Some inward agitations thence are brought,
Whate'er their office.

[1850 *Prelude* xii.292-333]

The secular and naturalistic frame of what is recorded remains intact. Yet the experience is comparable in more than its aura to what motivates prophecy. Though there is no intervention of vision or voice, there is something like a special, burdened relation to time. Wordsworth called the episode a "spot of time," to indicate that it stood out, spotlike, in his consciousness of time, that it merged sensation of place and sensation of time (so that time was *placed*), even that it allowed him to physically perceive or "spot" time.

The boy on the summit, overlooking the meeting point of two highways, and stationed between something immobile on his right hand and his left, is, as it were, at the center of a stark clock. Yet the question, How long? if it rises within him, remains mute. It certainly does not surface with the ghostly, prophetic dimension that invests it later. At this point there is simply a boy's impatient hope, "anxiety of hope," as the poet calls it (l.313), a straining of eye and mind that corresponds to the "far-stretched" perspective of the roads. But the father's death, which supervenes as an "event" (l.309), converts that moment of hope into an ominous, even murderous anticipation.

In retrospect, then, a perfectly ordinary mood is seen to involve a sin against time. The boy's "anxiety of hope," his wish for time to pass (both the "dreary time" of school and now of watching and waiting) seems to find retributive fulfillment when the father's life is cut short ten days later. The aftermath points to something unconscious in the first instance but manifest and punishing now. The child feels that his "desires" have been "corrected" by God. What desires could they be except fits of extreme—apocalyptic—impatience, brought on by the very patience or dreary sufferance of nature, of sheep and blasted tree? That the boy bowed low to God, who corrected his desires, evokes a human and orthodox version of nature's own passion.

A similar correction may be the subject of "A slumber did my spirit seal," where a milder sin against time, the delusion that the loved one is a "thing" exempt from the touch of years, is revealed when she dies and becomes a "thing" in fact. The fulfillment of the hope corrects it, as in certain fairy tales. In Wordsworth, hope or delusion always involves the hypnotic elision of time by an imagination drawn toward the "bleak music" of nature—of a powerfully inarticulate nature.

Yet in both representations, that of the death of the father and that of the death of the beloved, there is no hint of anything that would compel the mind to link the two terms, hope against time and its peculiar fulfillment. The link remains inarticulate, like nature itself. A first memory is interpreted by a second: the "event" clarifies an ordinary emotion by suggesting its apocalyptic vigor. But the apocalyptic mode, as Martin Buber remarked, is not the prophetic. Wordsworth's spots of time are said to renew time rather than to hasten its end. A wish for the end to come, for time to pass absolutely, cannot explain what brought the two happenings together, causally, superstitiously, or by a *vaticinum ex eventu.*

Perhaps the apocalyptic wish so compressed the element of time that something like a "gravitation" effect was produced, whereby unrelated incidents fell toward each other. It is, in any case, this process of conjuncture or binding that is mysterious. Not only for the reader but for Wordsworth himself. A more explicit revelation of the binding power had occurred after the death of the poet's mother. Wordsworth's "For now a trouble came into my mind / From unknown causes" (1850 *Prelude* ii.276–77) refers to an expectation that when his mother died the world would collapse. Instead it remains intact and attractive.

> I was left alone
> Seeking the visible world, nor knowing why.
> The props of my affection were removed,
> And yet the building stood, as if sustained
> By its own spirit!
> [1850 *Prelude* ii.277–81]

What he had previously named, describing the relationship between mother and infant, "the gravitation and the filial bond," continues to operate without the mother. This event contrary to expectation is the "trouble"; and the "unknown causes" allude to the gravitation, or glue or binding, that mysteriously sustains nature, and draws the child to it in the mother's absence. Even loss binds; and a paradox emerges which focuses on the fixative rather than fixating power of catastrophe, on the nourishing and reparative quality of the "trouble." Wordsworth, too benevolent perhaps, suggests that time itself is being repaired: that the pressure of eternity on thought (the parent's death) creates an "eternity of thought" (1850 *Prelude* i.402). The survivor knows that the burden of the mystery can be borne, that there is time for thought.

Whether or not, then, we understand Wordsworth's experience fully, the "spots of time" describe a trauma, a lesion in the fabric of time, or more precisely, the trouble this lesion produces and which shows itself as an extreme consciousness of time. Not only is there an untimely death in the case of the father, but it follows too fast on the boy's return home. As in *Hamlet,* "The time is out of joint. O cursed spite / That ever I was born to set it right!" The righting of the injury somehow falls to the poet. "Future restoration" (1850 *Prelude* xii.286), perhaps in the double sense of a restoration of the future as well as of a restoration still to come, is the task he sets himself.[1]

---

[1]Ordinary language, like ordinary incident, does indeed become very condensed and tricky here. "Thither I repaired," writes Wordsworth of the crag (l.296), and again, toward the end, "to which I oft repaired" (l.325), referring to the voluntary, sometimes involuntary, return of memory to the haunting scene. This "repaired" means simply "to go," the "re-" functioning as an intensifying particle. But in the second use of the word, the "re-" inclines the word toward its original sense of "return," or more specifically, "return to one's native country," *repatriare.* So that the first "repaired" may already contain proleptically the sense of returning to the father's house: climbing the crag is the first step in a conscious yet unconscious desire to overgo time and repatriate oneself, return home, to the father. The relation of "repair" to its etymological source is as tacit as unconscious process; so it may simply be a sport of language that when Wordsworth introduces the notion of "spots of time" a hundred or so lines before this, he also uses the word, though in its other root meaning of "restore," from *reparare:*

> There are in our existence spots of time,
> That with distinct pre-eminence retain
> A renovating virtue, whence, depressed
> By false opinion and contentious thought,
> Or aught of heavier or more deadly weight,
> In trivial occupations, and the round
> Of ordinary intercourse, our minds
> Are nourished and invisibly repaired;
> [1850 *Prelude* xii.208-15]

Though the young Wordsworth repairs to that which should nourish and repair (his father's house), he finds on the crag houseless or homeless phenomena, which hint at a stationary and endless patience. Whether "repair" may also have echoed in Wordsworth's mind as the re-pairing of man and nature (ll.298-302, which call hawthorn and sheep his "companions," as well as "kindred" [l.324], suggest his integration into a nonhuman family at the very point that the human one seems to fall away) must be left as moot as the foregoing speculations. The latter may suggest, however, not only the overdetermination of Wordsworth's deceptively translucent diction, but the consistency of his wish to join together what has been parted.

Prophecy, then, would seem to be anti-apocalyptic in seeking a "future restoration," or time for thought. But time, in Wordsworth, is also language, or what the Intimations Ode calls "timely utterance." That phrase contains both threat and promise. It suggests the urgent pressure that gives rise to speech; it also suggests that an animate response, and a harmonious one, is possible, as in Milton's "answerable style," or the pastoral cliché of woods and waters mourning, rejoicing or echoing in timely fashion the poet's mode. Ruskin referred to it as the pathetic fallacy but Abraham Heschel will make pathos, in that large sense, the very characteristic of prophetic language.

More radically still "timely utterance" means an utterance, such as prophecy, or prophetic poetry, which founds or repairs time. The prophet utters time in its ambiguity: as the undesired mediation, which prevents fusion, but also destruction. It prevents fusion by intruding the voice of the poet, his troubled heart, his fear of or flight from "power"; it prevents destruction by delaying God's decree or personally mediating it. Wordsworth speaks scrupulous words despite his sympathy with power and his attraction to the muteness or closure foreseen. By intertextual bonding, by words within words or words against words, he reminds us one more time of time.

We cannot evade the fact that the anxious waiting and the father's death are joined by what can only be called a "blast of harmony." The two moments are harmonized, but the copula is poetic as well as prophetic. For the conjunction of these contiguous yet disparate happenings into a "kindred" form is due to a "working of the spirit" that must be equated with poetry itself. While in the boy of thirteen the process of joining may have been instinctual, the poet recollects the past event as still working itself out; the incident demonstrated so forceful a visiting of imaginative power that later thought is never free of it. What is remarkable in this type-incident—and so remarkable that it keeps "working" on the mind "to this very time"—is not only the "coadunation," as Coleridge would have said, or "In-Eins-

Bildung" (his false etymology for the German *Einbildungskraft,* or imagination), but also that it is a "blast," that the workmanship reconciling the discordant elements anticipates a final, awesome unification. Hope is always "anxious" in that it foresees not just unity but also the power needed to achieve unity, to blast things into that state. The fear, then, that mingles with apocalyptic hope also stills it, or brings it close to "that peace / Which passeth understanding" (1850 *Prelude* xiv.126–27), because of the uncertain, terrible nature of this final bonding, which evokes in the episode on the crag a bleak and bleating music and images of stunned, warped, blasted, inarticulate being.

3

I turn to the climatic episode of *The Prelude,* the ascent of Snowdon in Book xiv. Disregarding all but its barest structure, we see that it again presents a sequence of two moments curiously harmonized. The theme of time enters *as elided* when the moon breaks through the mist and into the absorbed mind of the climber. "Nor was time given to ask or learn the cause, / For instantly a light upon the turf / Fell like a flash . . ." (xiv.37–39). This moment of prevenient light is followed as suddenly by a wild blast of music: the roar of waters through a rift in the mist. The second act or "event" is here an actual sound, separated off from sight and almost hypostatized as a sound. It is quite literally a "blast of harmony": "The roar of waters . . . roaring with one voice."

The appearance of the moon out of the mist is not, however, as unmotivated as might appear. It realizes an unuttered wish, "Let there be light," as the poet climbs through the darkness to "see the sun rise." Spotting the moon fulfills his hope in an unexpected way, which also foreshortens time. The mind of the poet is disoriented; but then time is lengthened as the sight of the moonstruck scene takes over in a kind of silent harmonization. If my hypothesis is correct, there is something truly magical here. The effect ("And there was light") utters the cause—that is, utters the scriptural text ("Let there be light") lodging as desire in the poet. Silence emits a "sound of harmony" (xiv.98–99) analogous to the music of the spheres. Not the poet but heaven itself declares the glory, the "And there was light" as "night unto night showeth knowledge." Wordsworth seems to behold visibly the "timely utterance" with which Genesis begins—the very harmony between cause and effect, between fiat and actualizing response—and this spectacle seems to be so ghostly a projection of nature itself (rather than of his own excited mind) that he claims it was "given to spirits of the night" and only by chance to the three human spectators (xiv.63–65).

Yet if the first act of the vision proper proves deceptive, because its motivation, which is a scriptural text, or the authority of that text, or the poet's desire to recapture that fiat power, remains silent and inward, the second act, which is the rising of the voice of the waters, also provides deceptive, even as it falsifies the first. The sound of the waters (though apparently unheard) must have been there all along, so that what is shown up by the vision's second act is a premature harmonizing of the landscape by the majestic moon: by that time-subduing object all sublime. Time also becomes a function of the desire for harmony as imagination now foreshortens and now enthrones the passing moment, or, to quote one of many variants, "so moulds, exalts, indues, combines, / Impregnates, separates, adds, takes away / And makes one object sway another so . . ." In the poet's commentary there is a further attempt at harmonizing, when moon and roaring waters are typified as correlative acts, the possessions of a mind

> That feeds upon infinity, that broods
> Over the dark abyss, intent to hear
> Its voices issuing forth to silent light
> In one continuous stream
>
> [xiv.71–74]

[29]

An image of communion and continuity is projected which the syntax partially subverts, for "its" remains ambiguous, and we cannot say for sure whether the voices belong to the dark abyss or the heavenly mind. What remains of this rich confusion are partial and contradictory structures of unification, which meet us "at every turn" in the "narrow rent" of the text, and add up less to a "chorus of infinity" than again to a "blast of harmony."

4

For prophet as for poet the ideal is "timely utterance," yet what we actually receive is a "blast of harmony." In Jeremiah a double pressure is exerted, of time on the prophet and of the prophet on time. The urgency of "timely utterance" cuts both ways. Moreover, while the prophet's words must harmonize with events, before or after the event, the word itself is viewed as an event that must harmonize with itself, or with its imputed source in God and the prophets. A passage such as Jeremiah 23:9–11 describes the impact of the God-word in terms that not only are conventionally ecstatic but also suggest the difficulty of reading the signs of authority properly, and distinguishing true from false prophet. "Adultery" seems to have moved into the word-event itself.

> Concerning the prophets:
> My heart is broken within me,
> all my bones shake;
> I am like a drunken man,
> like man overcome by wine,
> because of the LORD
> and because of his holy words.
> For the land is full of adulterers;
> because of the curse the land mourns. . . .

The time frame becomes very complex, then. On an obvious level the God-word as threat or promise is interpreted and reinterpreted in the light of history, so that Jeremiah's pronouncements are immediately set in their time. "The words of Jeremiah, the son of Hilkiah . . . to whom the word of the Lord came in the days of Josiah . . ." The ending *jah*, meaning "God," reveals from within these destined names the pressure for riming events with God. Jeremiah's prophecies are political suasions having to do with Israel's precarious position between Babylon on one border and Egypt on the other in the years before the destruction of Jerusalem by Nebuchadnezzar. The very survival of Israel is in question; and the prophet is perforce a political analyst as well as a divine spokesman. He speaks at risk not only in the hearing of God but also in that of Pashur, who beat him and put him in the stocks (20:1-4), in that of so-called friends who whisper "Denounce him to Pashur," and in that of King Zedekiah, the son of Josiah, king of Judah, who sends Pashur (the same or another) to Jeremiah, saying, "Inquire of the Lord for us" about Nebuchadnezzar, king of Babylon (21:1-3).

On another level, however, since the book of Jeremiah knows that the outcome is "the captivity of Jerusalem" (1:3), a question arises as to the later force of such prophecy. Near the onset of Jeremiah's career a manuscript of what may have been a version of Deuteronomy was found, and a dedication ceremony took place which pledged Judah once more to the covenant. The issue of the covenant—whether it is broken, or can ever be broken—and the part played in this issue by the survival of a book such as Jeremiah's own is another aspect of the prophet's utterance. Can one praise God yet curse oneself as the bearer of his word (20:13-14)? Or can Judah follow God into the wilderness once more, showing the same devotion as when it was a bride (2:2)? "I utter what was only in view of what will be. . . . What is realized in my history is not the past definite of what was, since it is no more, or even the present perfect of what has been in what I am, but the future anterior of what I shall have been for what I am in the process of becoming." That is Jacques Lacan on the function of language.

Indeed, the contradictions that beset "timely utterance" are so great that a reversal occurs which discloses one of the founding metaphors of literature. When Jacques Lacan writes that "symbols . . . envelop the life of man in a network so total that they join together, before he comes into the world, those who are going to engender him 'by flesh and blood'; so total that they bring to his birth, along with the gifts of the stars, if not with the gifts of the fairies, the shape of his destiny; so total that they give the words that will make him faithful or renegade, the law of the acts that will follow him right to the very place where he *is* not yet and even beyond his death; and so total that through them his end finds its meaning in the last judgement, where the Word absolves his being or condemns it," he is still elaborating Jeremiah 1:4. "Now the word of the LORD came to me saying, 'Before I formed you in the womb I knew you, and before you were born I consecrated you; I appointed you a prophet to the nations.'" This predestination by the word and unto the word— the "imperative of the Word," as Lacan also calls it, in a shorthand that alludes to the later tradition of the Logos—is then reinforced by Jeremiah 1:11-12. "And the word of the LORD came to me saying, 'Jeremiah, what do you see?' And I said, 'I see a rod of almond.' Then the LORD said to me, 'You have seen well, for I am watching over my word to perform it.'"

Here the pun of "rod of almond" (*makel shaqued*) and "[I am] watching" (*shoqued*) is more, surely, than a mnemonic or overdetermined linguistic device: it is a rebus that suggests the actualizing or performative relationship between words and things implied by the admonition: "I am watching over my word to perform it." The admonition is addressed to the prophet, in whose care the word is, and through him to the nation; while the very image of the rod of almond projects not only a reconciliation of contraries, of punishment (rod) and pastoral peace (almond), but the entire problem of timely utterance, since the almond tree blossoms unseasonably early and is as exposed to blasting as is the prophet, who seeks to avoid premature speech:

"Ah, Lord God! Behold, I do not know how to speak, for I am only a child." The forcible harmonizing of *shaqued* and *shoqued*, the pressure of that pun, or the emblematic abuse of a pastoral image, alerts us to the difficult pathos of prophetic speech. What does "watching over the word" involve? The prophets are politically and psychically in such a pressure-cooker situation ("I see a boiling pot," Jeremiah 1:13) that a powerful contamination occurs. Their words cannot always be distinguished from those of God in terms of who is speaking. The prophet identifies now with God and now with his people; moreover, his only way of arguing with the Lord is through words and figures given by the latter. Lacan would say that there is an inevitable inmixing of the Discourse of the Other. Jeremiah argues with God in God's language; and such scripture formulas as "according to thy word" recall this confused and indeterminate situation.

When, in famous lyric verses, Jeremiah admits that he cannot speak without shouting, and what he shouts is "violence and destruction" (20:8), it is as if the God-word itself had suffered a crisis of reference. For this typical warning is now directed not against Israel but against God: it refers to the condition of the prophet who feels betrayed as well as endangered. Jeremiah's hymn begins: "O Lord, you seduced me, and I was seduced," where "seduce," *pittiytani,* can mean both sexual enticement and spiritual deception—as by false prophets. No wonder that at the end of this hymn, the most formal and personal in the entire book, there is a surprising and unmotivated turn from blessing ("Sing to the LORD; praise the LORD") to cursing ("Cursed be the day on which I was born!" 20:13-18). However conventional such a curse may be, and we find a famous instance in Job, it cannot but be read in conjunction with "Before I formed you in the womb I knew you." Jeremiah's "Cursed be the day" is a Caliban moment; God has taught the prophet to speak, and so to curse; or it is a Hamlet moment, the prophet being "cursed" by his election to set the time right. But more important, the curse is the word itself, the violence done by it to the prophet. He feels it in his heart and bones as a burning fire (20:9). The word that knew him before he was conceived has displaced father and mother as begetter: when he curses his birth his word really curses the word. Jeremiah is not given time to develop; he is hurled untimely into the word. The words of the prophet and the words of God can be one only through that "blast of harmony" of which Wordsworth's dream still gives an inkling.

5

When even an intelligent contemporary discussion of "The Prophets as Poets" talks of a "symphony of the effective word" and "the gradual union of person and word," and sees prophecy advancing historically from "word as pointer to word as the thing itself," it adopts metaphors as solutions. The animating fiat spoken by God in the book of Genesis, which founds the harmonious correspondence of creative principle (word) and created product (thing), is literalized by a leap of faith on the part of the intelligent contemporary reader.

Yet with some exceptions—Wolfgang Binder and Peter Szondi on the language of Hölderlin, Erich Auerbach on Dante and figural typology, Northrop Frye on Blake, M. H. Abrams and E. S. Shaffer on the Romantics, Stanley Cavell on Thoreau—it is not the literary critics but the biblical scholars who have raised the issue of secularization (or, what affinity is there between secular and sacred word?) to a level where it is more than a problem in commuting: how to get from there to here, or vice versa. Since Ambrose and Augustine, and again since the Romantic era, biblical criticism has developed together with literary criticism; and still we are only beginning to appreciate their mutual concerns.

It is no accident that the career of Northrop Frye has promised to culminate in an Anatomy of the Bible, or in a summa of structural principles that could harmonize the two bodies of the logos: scripture and literature. By labeling an essay "The Poetics of Prophecy," I may seem to be going in the same direction, and I certainly wish to; yet I think that the relationship between *poetics* and *prophetics* cannot be so easily accommodated. The work of detail, or close reading, ever remains, and quite possibly as a task without an ending. Even when we seek to climb to a prospect where secular and sacred hermeneutics meet on some windy crag, we continue to face a number of unresolved questions that at once plague and animate the thinking critic.

One question is the status of figures. They seem to persist in language as indefeasible sedimentations or as recurrent necessity, long after the megaphone of prophetic style. Moreover, because of the priority and survival of "primitive" or "oriental" figuration, such distinctions as Coleridge's between fancy and imagination tend to become the problem they were meant to resolve. Strong figurative expression does not reconcile particular and universal, or show the translucence of the universal in the concrete: there is such stress and strain that even when theorists value one mode of imaginative embodiment over another—as symbol over allegory or metaphysical wit—they admit the persistence and sometimes explosive concurrence of the archaic or depreciated form.

Another important question is the status of written texts in the life of society or the life of the mind. Almost every tradition influenced by Christianity has aspired to a spiritualization of the word, its transformation and even disappearance as it passes from "word as pointer to word as thing itself." A logocentric or incarnationist thesis of this kind haunts the fringes of most studies of literature, and explains the welcome accorded at present to semiotic counterperspectives. Textual reality, obviously, is more complex, undecidable, and lasting than any such dogma; and the dogma itself is merely inferred from historically ramified texts.

A last question concerns intertextuality. From the perspective of scripture intertextuality is related to canon formation, or the process of authority by which the bibles (*biblia*) we call the Bible were unified. The impact of scripture on literature includes the concept of (1) peremptory or preemptive texts and (2) interpreters who find the unifying principle that could join books into a canon of classics. From a secular perspective these books, whether classified as literature or as scripture, have force but no authority; and to bring them together into some sort of canon is the coup of the critic, who harmonizes them by the force of his own text. His work reveals not their canonicity but rather their intertextuality; and the most suggestive theory along these lines has been that of Harold Bloom.

The impact, according to him, of a preemptive poem on a later one is always "revisionary": the one lives the other's death, deviating its meaning, diverting its strength, creating an inescapable orbit. "Revisionary" suggests, therefore, a relationship of force: again, a blast of harmony rather than a natural or authoritative unification.

For a reason not entirely clear to me, Bloom wishes to establish English poetry after Milton as a Milton satellite. Milton becomes a scripture substitute with the impressive and oppressive influence of scripture itself. Later poets must harmonize with Milton, willingly or unwillingly: even their deviations are explained by attempts to escape the Milton orbit. Yet I have shown that Wordsworth may imitate a scripture text ("Let there be light") with a power of deviousness that is totally un-Miltonic. Milton and Nature, Wordsworth saw, were not the same. His return to scripture is not to its precise verbal content, though it is an implicit content (Genesis, light, voice) that infuses the texture of the vision on Snowdon. The form of the fiat, however, predominates over its content; and what we are given to see is not scripture reenacted or imaginatively revised—new testamented—but the unuttered fiat in its silent yet all-subduing aspect. What Wordsworth names and represents as Nature is the fiat power working tacitly and harmoniously, reconciling discordant elements, building up the mind and perhaps the cosmos itself.

Snowdon's Miltonic echoes, therefore, which recapitulate a portion of the story of creation as retold in the seventh book of *Paradise Lost,* are allusions whose status is as hard to gauge as those to *Hamlet* in the "spot of time" referring to the father's death. The converging highways, moreover, in that spot of time could lead the contemporary reader (perhaps via Freud) to Oedipus, so that a question arises on the relation of revisionary to hermeneutic perspectives, making the intertextual map more tricky still. Yet Wordsworth's vision, natural rather than textual in its apparent motivation, can still be called revisionary because a prior and seminal text may be hypothetically reconstituted.

The act of reconstitution, however, now includes the reader in a specific and definable way. The *poet* as reader is shown to have discovered from within himself, and so recreated, a scripture text. The *interpreter* as reader has shown the capacity of a "secular" text to yield a "sacred" intuition by a literary act of understanding that cannot be divided into those categories. On the level of interpretation, therefore, we move toward what Schleiermacher called *Verstehen,* on the basis of which a hermeneutic is projected that seeks to transcend the dichotomizing of religious and nonreligious modes of understanding and of earlier (prophetic) and later (poetic-visionary) texts.

6

Returning a last time to Wordsworth: much remains to be said concerning the "gravitation and the filial bond" that links earlier visionary texts to his own. The reader, in any case, also moves in a certain gravitational field; and I have kept myself from being pulled toward a Freudian explanation of the nexus between the boy's "anxiety of hope" and the guilty, affective inscription on his mind of a natural scene. My only finding is that should a God-word precede in Wordsworth, it is rarely foregrounded, but tends to be part of the poem's ground as an inarticulate, homeless or ghostly, sound. It becomes, to use one of his own expressions, an "inland murmur."

In the second act of Snowdon this sound comes out of the deep and is suddenly the very subject, the "Imagination of the whole" (1805 *Prelude* xiii.65). Though the text behind that sound cannot be specified, it is most probably the word within the word, the Word that was in the Beginning (John 1:1), and which uttered as from chaos, "Let there be light." In Milton the first words of the "Omnific Word" are "Silence, ye troubl'd Waves, and thou Deep, peace" (*Paradise Lost* vii.216), a proto-fiat Wordsworth may have absorbed into his vision of silence followed by his more radical vision of the power in sound.

When the poet writes, "The sounding cataract haunted me like a passion" ("Tintern Abbey"), there is again no sense of a proof text of any kind. We recognize a congruity of theme between this waterfall and the "roar of waters" heard on Snowdon, and perhaps associate both with Psalm 42: "Deep calls unto deep at the thunder of thy cataracts." Such allusions may exist, but they are "tidings" born on the wave of natural experience. Yet a prophetic text does enter once more in the way we have learned to understand. The word "passion," by being deprived of specific reference, turns back on itself, as if it contained a muted or mutilated meaning. By a path more devious than I can trace, the reader recovers for "passion" its etymological sense of "passio"—and the word begins to embrace the pathos of prophetic speech, or a suffering idiom that is strongly inarticulate or musical, like the "earnest expectation of the creature . . . subjected . . . in hope" of which Paul writes in Romans (8:19–20), like sheep, blasted tree, and the boy who waits with them, and the barely speaking figures that inhabit the poet's imagination. The event, in Wordsworth, is the word of connection itself, a word event (the poem) that would repair the bond between human hopes and a mutely remonstrant nature, "subjected in hope."

"Do you know the language of the old belief?" asks Robert

Duncan. "The wild boar too / turns a human face." Today the hope in such a turning includes the very possibility of using such language. A mighty scheme not of truth but of troth—of trusting the old language, its pathos, its animism, its fallacious figures—is what connects poet and prophet. When Wordsworth apostrophizes nature at the end of the Intimations Ode, he still writes in the old language, yet how precariously, as he turns toward what is turning away:

> And O, ye Fountains, Meadows, Hills and Groves,
> Forebode not any severing of our loves!

Bibliographical Note

The locus classicus of Coleridgean poetics is found in Chapters 13 and 14 of the *Biographia Literaria* (1818), "On the Imagination, or Esemplastic Power," etc. *Aids to Reflection* (1824) and a mass of miscellaneous lectures and readings contain many subtle and varying attempts to distinguish between symbolical and allegorical, analogous and metaphorical language, and so forth. Coleridge's reflections on the subject of style and unity are much more intricate than my general comment suggests; see, for one example, "On Style," reprinted in *Coleridge's Miscellaneous Criticism*, ed. T. M. Raysor (Cambridge, Mass., 1936), pages 214–17. Yet even there German-type speculation is mixed with practical and preacherly admonition. The major German influence in regard to art, revelation, and the question of unity (or "identity philosophy") was, of course, Schelling. Martin Buber's distinction between apocalyptic and prophetic is made in "Prophecy, Apocalyptic, and the Historical Hour," in *On the Bible* (New York, 1968). For Abraham Heschel on pathos, see *The Prophets* (New York, 1962). The intelligent contemporary discussion on prophets as poets is in David Robertson's chapter of that title in *The Old Testament and the Literary Critic* (Philadelphia, 1977). Robertson acknowledges his debt to Gerhard von Rad's *Old Tes-*

tament Theology, volume 2. To the literary scholars mentioned in my essay, I should add Paul de Man's and Angus Fletcher's work on the theory of allegory; Walter Benjamin's seminal reconsideration of baroque allegory in *The Origin of German Tragic Drama* (originally published in 1928); and articles by Robert W. Funk on the parable in the New Testament and in Kafka. Frank Kermode is also working on the parable and has begun publishing on the idea of canon formation. Elinor Shaffer's *Kubla Khan and the Fall of Jerusalem* (Cambridge, England, 1976) links up more specifically than Basil Willey movements in Bible criticism and considerations of literary form. Her chapter entitled "The Visionary Character" is especially valuable in summarizing the movement of thought whereby poets, critics, and theologians came to consider Holy Writ as composed of different poetic and narrative genres, and faced the question of how to value nonapostolic (generally "apocalyptic" rather than "prophetic") visionariness. My quotations from Jacques Lacan can be found in *Ecrits: A Selection* (New York, 1977), pages 68 and 86. The issue of secularization in literary history is central to M. H. Abrams' *Natural Supernaturalism* (1971) and has elicited, in the Anglo-American domain, many partial theories from Matthew Arnold to Daniel Bell. Stanley Cavell's *The Senses of Walden* (1971) reveals a Wordsworthian type of underwriting in Thoreau, and one so consistent in its allusions to earlier epics and scriptures that *Walden* begins to emerge as a sacred book.

As with the Silence of the Thought

JONATHAN WORDSWORTH

"Oh, why hath not the mind," Wordsworth writes in February 1804, the most creative month of his life—

> Oh, why hath not the mind
> Some element to stamp her image on
> In nature somewhat nearer to her own?[1]

The lines come from the clumsy, half-powerful opening paragraph of *Prelude*, Book V, in which the poet grieves with Hamlet for the state of man as "paramount creature," but grieves more especially for the fate of his writings—"The consecrated works of bard and sage." At the other end of the book is a passage quite as idiosyncratic in which Wordsworth, who has been unable to convince himself or his audience of the importance of literature as such in his education, comes out with the sudden, astonishing statement:

[1]1805 *Prelude*, v.44–46; *Prelude* quotations are drawn from the Norton Critical Edition of *The Prelude, 1799, 1805, 1850* (New York, 1979), ed. Jonathan Wordsworth, M. H. Abrams, and Stephen Gill. Lines are cited always from the earliest text in which they occur. For other Wordsworth texts, quotations are drawn from my forthcoming chronological edition and references given for convenience to sources where the poetry may already be found in its original form.

[41]

JONATHAN WORDSWORTH .

Visionary Power
Attends upon the motions of the winds
Embodied in the mystery of words . . .
[*1805*, v.619-21]

In "The Correspondent Breeze," M. H. Abrams has of course traced the visionary power of winds in Romantic metaphor;[2] taking as my starting point the two passages quoted, I should like in a far more limited way to play the game of following associations, and see if perhaps they lead to a greater sense of the power embodied in Wordsworth's language, the reasons that lie beneath his peculiar choice and use of certain words and clusters of words.

Back in 1799 Wordsworth had used the image of stamping in a rather more expected way:

> Yes, I remember when the changeful earth
> And twice five seasons on my mind had stamped
> The faces of the moving year . . .
> [*1799*, i.391-93]

Wordsworth is not at his most original, yet for all their conventionality, his lines are saved from tedium by their curious and characteristic physical emphasis. The child is acquiring the "real solid world / Of images" (*1805*, viii.604-5) that will "steady" him in adult life, and seasonal landscapes are printed onto his mind like a series of woodcuts. The extent to which visual memory, and the experience it records, is solid in this poetry—actually *weighty*—is quite extraordinary. One is not too surprised to hear of "The heavy weight of many a weary day" (*1805*, i.24), or the weight of ages, custom, unintelligibility, but Wordsworth can feel a weight too in liberty, joy, pleasure, good humor, even in chance desires. All these are sustained by the mind; collectively

[2]M. H. Abrams, "The Correspondent Breeze: A Romantic Metaphor," *Kenyon Review*, 19 (1957), 113-30; revised version in *English Romantic Poets*, ed. M. H. Abrams. 2d ed. (London, Oxford, New York, 1975), pp. 37-54.

they are "life's mysterious weight," "the burthen of the mystery."
Even where moods and states of mind in Wordsworth's poetry
do not have palpable weight, the sense of their physical presence
is exceptionally strong. Imagination *comes athwart* the poet,
memory *rises up against him,* restoration comes

> Like an intruder knocking at the door
> Of unacknowledged weariness . . .
> [*1805*, iv.147-48]

and terrors of the past can actually be touched:

> I thought of those September massacres,
> Divided from me by a little month,
> And felt and touched them, a substantial dread
> [*1805*, x.64-66]

Lacking Wordsworth's "more than usual organic sensibility," at
times we probably read more abstractly than he expected. The
"high objects" with which the child's emotions are intertwined in
The Prelude (*1799*, i.136) are not exalted aims, but chunks of the
countryside—probably in fact mountains, with an unconscious
pun on "high." "Things," too, tend to have a very concrete
thingness: who else would call man a "thinking thing"? And if
one continues the *Tintern Abbey* quotation,

> A motion and a spirit that impels
> All thinking things, all objects of all thought,
> And rolls through all things[3]

it is clear that Wordsworth, as himself a "thinking thing," has in
mind God's presence not in space, infinity, eternity, but in the
separate blockish units of the material world. When he sees "into
the life of things," the last word should be taking a lot of the
stress.

[3]Ll. 101-3; all quotations from *Lyrical Ballads* and the Preface are drawn from
the edition of R. L. Brett and A. R. Jones (new and revised impression, London,
1965).

[43]

Similarly, it is doubtful whether the many printing images of Wordsworth's poetry are felt with their original force, whether we always receive, and carry away, the right impression:

> In these my lonely wanderings I perceived
> What mighty objects do *impress* their forms
> To build up this our intellectual being . . .[4]

> deep feelings had *impressed*
> Great objects on his mind with portraiture
> And colour so distinct that on his mind
> They lay like substances . . .[5]

The objects don't get *into* the memory, *into* the mind, they lie upon it, retaining not just form, but substance. As Wordsworth elsewhere puts it, they are "in their *substantial* lineaments / Depicted" (*1799*, i.430–31). Given the "ennobling interchange / Of action from within and from without" (*1805*, xii.376–77), one should perhaps expect that this printing process will go two ways. Hills that have impressed upon the mind of Michael "So many incidents . . . Of hardship, skill or courage, joy or fear" become themselves a book preserving the memory of animals that he has saved (ll.68–74). More numinous, yet in its different way as typically Wordsworthian, is the "peak / Familiar with forgotten years"

> which shews
> *Inscribed, as with the silence of the thought,*
> Upon its bleak and visionary sides
> The history of many a winter storm
> Or obscure records of the path of fire
> [*Pedlar*, ll. 169–73]

[4]Rivers (Oswald in the later text) speaking in *The Borderers*, IV.ii.133–35; quoted from Dove Cottage MS. 23. Where quotations in this paper are italicized, the italics are mine unless identified by the author's initials.

[5]*The Pedlar*, ll.30–33; quotations from *The Ruined Cottage* and *The Pedlar* are drawn from Jonathan Wordsworth, *The Music of Humanity* (London and New York, 1969).

And of course there are the "steep and lofty cliffs" of *Tintern Abbey*, which impress not upon the mind, but upon the wild secluded scene, *"Thoughts* of more deep seclusion" (ll.6–7). But even this is some way from the strange compelling wish that the mind of the poet himself might have

> Some element to stamp her image on
> In nature somewhat nearer to her own . . .

One can if one chooses give "nature" a capital *N*, and ask why the mind hasn't some element that is closer to her own *within the natural world* to print her image on. More probably Wordsworth meant some element that *in its own nature* was closer to the mind; but in fact the readings amount to very much the same. Either way he is asking, as no one else ever could or would have asked, why mind cannot print upon mind, why the human spirit in the grandeur and permanence of its achievement must be dependent upon such transient and destructible material as books and paper. Instead of asking with Keats and others why life cannot have the permanence of art, he is asking why art cannot have the permanence of life. Perhaps the passage should be given its fuller context: "A thought is with me sometimes," Wordsworth begins,

> and I say,
> 'Should earth by inward throes be wrenched throughout,
> Or fire be sent from far to wither all
> Her pleasant habitations, and dry up
> Old Ocean in his bed, left singed and bare,
> Yet would the living presence still subsist
> Victorious; and composure would ensue,
> And kindlings like the morning—presage sure,
> Though slow perhaps, of a returning day.'
> But all the meditations of mankind,
> Yea, all the adamantine holds of truth
> By reason built, or passion (which itself
> Is highest reason in a soul sublime),

> The consecrated words of bard or sage . . .
> Where would they be? *Oh, why hath not the mind*
> *Some element to stamp her image on*
> *In nature somewhat nearer to her own?*
> Why, gifted with such powers to send abroad
> Her spirit, must it lodge in shrines so frail?
> [*1805*, v.28-48]

Life it seems is indestructible. The embers of humanity—*Intimations* must have been completed this same month[6]—may be relied upon to rekindle. It is the works of bard and sage, consecrated at the altar of human achievement, that may perish. And so we get the dream of the Arab with his stone and shell, to which these are the introductory lines.

Can Wordsworth, one wonders, really be preoccupied with the transitoriness of books as such, or even of philosophy (the stone) and poetry (the shell) in their own right? His language in the introduction has about it a disproportionate intensity that will return at the end of the dream, where sympathy with the

> gentle dweller in the desert, crazed
> By love, and feeling, and internal thought
> Protracted among endless solitudes . . .

turns into a moment of strange imbalance:

> And I have scarcely pitied him, have felt
> A reverence for a being thus employed,
> And thought that in the blind and awful lair
> Of such a madness reason did lie couched.
> [*1805*, v.144-52]

One hasn't in the dream thought of the Arab as mad at all, and neither the associations of Don Quixote nor the poet's own identification have led one to think of his mind as a "blind and awful lair." The image is violent, shocking, an intrusion of personal

---

[6]February 1804.

terrors into poetry that has seemed to be decorous and assured. The poet sets out to tell us of an underlying reasonableness, and ends by portraying reason as a wild beast and the mind as its den. After Parson Adams, Uncle Toby, Matthew Bramble—not to mention Johnny Foy—there was no actual need to point to the Arab as a holy fool, but there was still less call to use such violent imagery in doing so. One is left wondering whether at some level Wordsworth was confronting the possibility that he himself could be mad, crazed by protracted internal thought, deluded in his mission and his aspirations.[7] Be that as it may, he goes on with exemplary neatness to tie the episode back to the point from which he started:

> I methinks
> Could share that maniac's anxiousness, could go
> Upon like errand. Oftentimes at least
> Me hath such deep entrancement half-possessed
> When I have held a volume in my hand—
> Poor earthly casket of immortal verse—
> Shakespeare or Milton, labourers divine.
> [*1805*, v.159–65]

It is interesting that the earthly casket should be virtually the same image as the shrines at the end of the introductory lines:

> Why, gifted with such powers to send abroad
> Her spirit, must it lodge in shrines so frail?
> [*1805*, v.47–48]

---

[7]For an alternative view, see Jonathan Bishop's conclusion in "Wordsworth and the 'Spots of Time'":

We may now paraphrase the dream as follows: 'If you choose poetry as a way of life, as you have done and are bound to do, you run the severe risk of being overwhelmed by the unconscious forces from which your poetry must derive its vital inspiration, and the significant portion of its subject matter; if you lose your nerve, you will find yourself "burying" your talent to escape the emotional turmoil it brings upon you.' [*ELH*, 26 (1959), 65, reprinted in *Wordsworth, "The Prelude": A Casebook*, ed. W. J. Harvey and Richard Gravil (1972), p. 153]

[47]

In each case, traditional metaphors for the soul and body are used instead for mind and book. Or is it merely for mind and book? In the dream, the shell that the Arab is trying to save is not just a book, but a god,

> yea many gods,
> Had voices more than all the winds, and was
> A joy, a consolation, and a hope.
> [*1805*, v.107–9]

The godlike property of the shell is to give form, meaning, without trammeling inspiration. If one puts it to one's ear one hears not language but articulate sounds, "A loud prophetic blast of harmony" that remains a blast though harmonious and fully comprehensible, "An ode in passion uttered" that achieves the structure of art without qualifying the passion. The stone that is likewise a book and represents philosophy, though said to be less important, turns out to have very much the same attribute, "wedd[ing] man to man by purest bond / Of nature, undisturbed by space or time" (*1805*, v.105–6)—dispensing, as the poet would ideally wish to be able to do, with limiting temporal bonds and connections.

If the wish that mind should be able to print upon mind is at some level a wish to remove the impediment of language, one is left asking how much *did* Wordsworth the poet distrust his medium—he was, after all, prone to make comments about "the sad incompetence of human speech" and the need for "Colours and words that are unknown to man" so that he could "paint the visionary dreariness" of experience. Some of his pronouncements make it all seem quite simple, a question merely of the writer's selecting that which is natural, and avoiding "those arbitrary connections of feelings and ideas with particular words, from which no man can altogether protect himself."[8] The poet "will feel that there is no necessity to trick out or to elevate Nature: and, the more industriously he applies this principle,

[8]Preface to *Lyrical Ballads* (1800), ed. Brett and Jones, p. 268.

the deeper will be his faith that no words, which his fancy or imagination can suggest, will be to be compared with those which are the emanations of reality and truth."[9]

Through a redefinition of David Hartley's millenarian claims, Wordsworth at the time of the Preface is able to think of writing as *positively* mechanical—a process in which the beneficent power of association, acting in both poet and audience, will of necessity lead to improvements. As is so often the case, it is the passage that qualifies a too-famous quotation that turns out to be most important:

> For all good poetry is the spontaneous overflow of powerful feelings; but though this be true, Poems to which any value can be attached, were never produced on any variety of subjects but by a man who possessed of more than usual organic sensibility had also thought long and deeply. For our continued influxes of feeling are modified and directed by our thoughts, which are indeed the representatives of all our past feelings; and as by contemplating the relation of these general representatives to each other, we discover what is really important to men, so by the repetition and continuance of this act feelings connected with important subjects will be nourished, till at length, if we be originally possessed of much organic sensibility, such habits of mind will be produced that by obeying blindly and mechanically the impulses of those habits we shall describe objects and utter sentiments of such a nature and in such connection with each other, that the understanding of the being to whom we address ourselves, if he be in a healthful state of association, must necessarily be in some degree enlightened, his taste exalted, and his affections ameliorated.[10]

"Or, in other words, association"—as Hartley comments in Part I of the *Observations on Man*—"has a tendency to reduce the state of those who have eaten of the tree of the knowledge of good and evil, back again into a paradisiacal one."[11]

A "healthful state of association" in the reader is especially

---

[9]Ibid. (1802), p. 257.

[10]Ibid. (1800), pp. 246–47.

[11]David Hartley, *Observations on Man* (1749), reissued with Notes by H. Pistorius (3 vols., 1791), I, 83.

important to Wordsworth's thinking: poetry must be creatively read as well as creatively written. Composition, he writes in the second of the 1810 *Essays on Epitaphs,* speaks from the "primary sensations of the human heart," and "unless correspondent ones listen promptly and submissively in the inner cell of the mind to whom it is addressed, the voice cannot be heard: its highest powers are wasted."[12] It seems as if the problem of inducing such a response, subduing association to his purposes, came to seem increasingly difficult. Language, he comments in 1815, is "a thing subject to endless fluctuations and arbitrary associations. The genius of the poet melts these down for his purpose; but they retain their shape and quality to him who is not capable of exerting, within his own mind, a corresponding energy" (*Essay, Supplementary to the Preface; Prose Works,* III, 82). As Stephen K. Land has remarked in his very useful article on "The Silent Poet," "Wordsworth's aim, for the theoretical purposes of poetry, is to divest language of all secondary associations and to confine (poetic) communication to the sphere governed by 'the primary laws of our nature'."[13] The depth of the poet's anxiety is brought out most clearly in a passage that a number of recent critics have cited, but none looked at very closely, from the third of the 1810 *Essays.* "Words are too awful an instrument for good and evil to be trifled with," Wordsworth begins impressively, "they hold above all other external powers a dominion over thoughts." "If words be not . . . an incarnation of the thought"—one hears the style becoming prophetic, sybilline, as he strives to express a feeling about the nature of language that once again is surely disproportionate—"then surely will they prove an ill gift; such a one as those poisoned vestments, read of in the stories of superstitious times, which had power to consume and to alienate from his right mind the victim who put them on. Language, if it do not uphold..." The tone has

---

[12]*The Prose Works of William Wordsworth,* ed. W. J. B. Owen and Jane Worthington Smyser (3 vols., Oxford, 1974), II, 70.
[13]*UTQ,* 42, no. 2 (Winter 1973), 164.

changed again. We are suddenly with the mother and her feeding child: "Language, if it do not uphold, and feed, and leave in quiet, like the power of gravitation or the air we breathe, is a counter-spirit" (violence returns), "unremittingly and noiselessly at work to derange, to subvert, to lay waste, to vitiate, and to dissolve" (*Prose Works,* II, 84–85).[14] Wordsworth's use of the term "incarnation"—which can after all imply exactly the dualism that he is here rejecting[15]—causes De Quincey to comment thirty years later, "Never in one word was so profound a truth conveyed." He is writing about style and subjectivity, and recalls what was apparently a conversation with the poet at the time of the *Essays on Epitaphs:*

> In saying this, we do but vary the form of what we once heard delivered on this subject by Mr. Wordsworth. His remark was by far the weightiest thing we ever heard on the subject of style; and it was this: that it is in the highest degree unphilosophic to call language or diction "the *dress* of thoughts" ... he would call it "the *incarnation* of thoughts" ... The truth is apparent on consideration: for, if language were merely a dress, then you could separate the two; you could lay the thoughts on the left hand, the language on the right. But, generally speaking, you can no more deal thus with poetic thoughts than you can with soul and body. The union is too subtle, the intertexture too ineffable,—each coexisting not merely *with* the other, but each *in* and *through* the other. An image, for instance, a single word, often enters into a thought as a constituent part. In short, the two elements are not united as a body with a separable dress, but as a mysterious incarnation.[16]

---

[14]This passage of course provides Frances Ferguson with her title, *Wordsworth: Language as Counter-Spirit* (New Haven and London, 1977). Her interest is much more theoretical than mine—much less concerned with the ways in which the poet *uses* language, both in his critical pronouncements and elsewhere—and I think there is room for us both.

[15]The metaphor of the body as clothing or containing the soul is implied, for instance, in the images of shrine and casket with which the Quixote dream begins and ends.

[16]*Collected Writings of Thomas De Quincey,* ed. David Masson (14 vols., Edinburgh, 1890), X, 229–30; the passage is quoted in large part in *Prose Works,* II, 114–15.

The emphasis on mystery is especially interesting—the coexistence of thought and language "*in* and *through*" each other. Professor Land has argued persuasively that Wordsworth "used the incarnation metaphor . . . with a clear awareness of its strong implied dualism";[17] but De Quincey is not at all often wrong about Wordsworth the writer, however resentful he may sometimes be of the man. We cannot know whether he had read the unpublished third *Essay* of 1810, or whether the conversation he recalls had placed incarnation in a similar context, but he surely provides the best possible gloss on Wordsworth's original definition.

"Words," to go back to the beginning of the poet's solemn warning, "are too awful an instrument for good and evil to be trifled with: they hold above all other external powers a dominion over thoughts." It is a remarkable statement, but not apparently a hasty one. Words have more power even than the primary external forces of Nature—more than "The mountain's outline and its steady form" which confer upon the mind a "simple grandeur," more than the crag, which, rising up between the steady outline and the stars, can chase a child across a lake, filling his mind with "grave / And serious thoughts," peopling it with alien forms, affecting his future development and future life. What is it that can give to language this extraordinary power?—and to Wordsworth's language in this instance such extraordinary vehemence? Two further cases of the word "incarnation" in his writing may be a help. The first belongs to *Prelude*, Book VII, and seems a little pedestrian. Wordsworth is recalling how very limited his response had been to drama. Even tragedy, it appears, had not passed "beyond the suburbs of [his] mind."[18] The actors and action seen at the theatre had been an "incarnation of the spirits that moved / Amid the poet's beauteous world" (vii.510-11)—presumably, that is, in Shakespeare's

---

[17]Stephen K. Land, "The Silent Poet," *UTQ*, 42, no. 2 (1973), 160.
[18]The image, from *Julius Caesar*, II.i.285-86, has a special appropriateness, as Wordsworth had been in London at the time.

beauteous world—but they had also been in their own right "gross realities." The world of imagination had been present to the mind only as a contrast. In the very ineptitude of the actors Wordsworth had recognized

> As by a glimpse, the things which [he] had shaped
> And yet not shaped, had seen and scarcely seen,
> Had felt, and thought of in [his] solitude.
>
> [*1805*, vii.514–17]

The solitary reading of Shakespeare had led to imaginative shapings that were necessarily imprecise—a creative fusion of things made, seen, felt, and thought. The dramatist's *words* had thus been successful in their incarnation of the ideal in a way that ceased to be possible when the world of imagination was too literally "embodied" in the theatre. But poetry too is circumscribed. The *Essay Supplementary to the Preface* of 1815 defines its powers and limitations in terms of an affinity with religion:

> The concerns of religion refer to indefinite objects, and are too weighty for the mind to support them without relieving itself by resting a great part of the burthen upon words and symbols. The commerce between man and his Maker cannot be carried on but by a process where much is represented in little, and the Infinite Being accommodates himself to a finite capacity. In all this may be perceived the affinity between religion and poetry . . . between religion, whose element is infinitude, and whose ultimate trust is the supreme of things, submitting herself to circumscription, and reconciled to substitutions; and poetry, ethereal and transcendent, yet incapable to sustain her existence without sensuous incarnation. [*Prose Works*, III, 65]

J. Hillis Miller, in his essay "The Stone and the Shell," has asked himself the question: "Does the meaning [in Wordsworth] pre-exist the signs for it, so that it is only expressed, copied or represented by them, or does it come into existence only in its signs? Does Word precede words, or is it the other way around?"[19] The answer must surely be yes, meaning does pre-exist, Word does precede words, at least insofar as what is being talked about is Wordsworth's most deeply felt, underlying attitudes toward language. The Word becomes incarnate in Christ; drama becomes incarnate in the actors; poetry, in its nature ideal, can *sustain* the existence it has in the imagination only through the "sensuous incarnation" of language. Words take on an extraordinary responsibility and extraordinary power. Only they can "fix in a visible home," endue "with a frame of outward life" the "phantoms of conceit" that float loose in the poet's mind, thus expressing and assuaging "The many feelings that oppressed [his] heart" (*1805*, i.127–33). Choice of language that is mere clothing to the thought is a betrayal of the original creative impulse, a denial of that which has been ethereal and transcendent. It can be seen as a settling for poetic diction, but where that term usually implies a language that is glossy and inert—and had indeed done so for Wordsworth himself in the 1802 Appendix to the Preface to *Lyrical Ballads*—the force that is evoked in the *Essay on Epitaphs* is active and threatening. To falsify is to surrender control over one's own mind. Falsification once accepted becomes indistinguishable from fact, becomes a habit, a way of thinking, a poison that maddens and seemingly lacks all antidote. In its way the force let loose resembles the apocalyptic dullness of *Dunciad*, Book IV, but it is felt as a personal fear: "a counter-spirit unremittingly and noiselessly at work to derange, to subvert, to lay waste, to vitiate, and to dissolve."

There is a sense in which this negative and negating power runs counter to the human spirit itself, but it is counter especially to the spirit of the poet's own creativity—the "plastic power" which in Part II of the 1799 *Prelude* is also personified,

---

[19]J. Hillis Miller, "The Stone and the Shell: The Problem of Poetic Form in Wordsworth's Dream of the Arab," in *Mouvements premiers: Etudes critiques offertes à Georges Poulet* (Paris, 1972), p. 126.

also maverick, also at work within the mind, and which
exemplifies the most confident, expansive moment in
Wordsworth's early relationship with Nature:

> A plastic power
> Abode with me, a forming hand, at times
> Rebellious, acting in a devious mood,
> A local spirit of its own, at war
> With general tendency, but for the most
> Subservient strictly to the external things
> With which it communed. An auxiliar light
> Came from my mind, which on the setting sun
> Bestowed new splendour; the melodious birds,
> The gentle breezes, fountains that ran on
> Murmuring so sweetly in themselves, obeyed
> A like dominion, and the midnight storm
> Grew darker in the presence of my eye.
>
> [*1799*, ii.411-23]

One spirit enhances everything it touches, the other lays waste,
subverts, dissolves; one plainly is the imagination, the other is its
daemonic antithesis. The "plastic power" is *of* the mind, and,
though displaying at times an autonomy, subservient on the
whole to the general forces of Nature; the "counter-spirit" is
external—words, after all, are common property—but may establish a hold *within* the mind as a result of creativity misused.

Behind the statement that "words hold above all other external powers a dominion over thoughts" is the poet's surprise that
any power outside the mind could be strong enough to dominate. "Great God," he wrote of the moment of entry into London at the end of *Prelude,* Book VIII,

> That aught *external* to the living mind
> Should have such mighty sway . . .
>
> [*1805*, viii.700-702]

We may be inclined with Coleridge to say that it didn't, that this
was a case in which

power streamed from [him], and [his] soul received
The light reflected as a light bestowed . . .
                    [*To William Wordsworth*, ll. 18–19]

but it does not alter the fact that the experience is *felt* to be
external. To continue the quotation,

                    yet so it was:
A weight of ages did at once descend
Upon my heart—no thought embodied, no
Distinct remembrances, but weight and power,
Power growing with the weight.
                    [*1805*, viii.702–6]

Power, as De Quincey points out, again thinking of Wordsworth,
though not this time referring to him directly, is the "exercise
and *expansion* [of the individual's] latent capacity of sympathy
with the infinite."[20] Power cannot stay still, and it has to find
expression. In the immediate experience there will be "no
thought embodied," but thought comes as a secondary stage,
and with it, if the process is uncontaminated, will come (to return to the *Essay on Epitaphs*) "expressions which are not what
the garb is to the body but what the body is to the soul, themselves a constituent part and power or function in the
thought . . ." (*Prose Works*, II, 84).[21]

If, as a critic, and presumably as a writer, one wishes to test
language to see if it is truly an incarnation, the second of the
1810 *Essays* tells us confidently that there is an "art of bringing
words rigorously to the test of thoughts; and these again to a

[20]*Collected Writings of Thomas De Quincey*, ed. Masson, XI, 56; compare
Wordsworth's own statement in the *Guide to the Lakes:* "Power awakes the sublime . . . when it arouses us to a sympathetic energy and calls upon the mind to
grasp at something towards which it can make approaches, but which it is incapable of attaining—yet so that it participates [the] force which is acting upon it"
(*Prose Works*, II, 354).
[21]Frances Ferguson seems to me much more pessimistic than the poet is himself. "Wordsworth," she writes, "posits the ideal of language as an incarnation
rather than a mere garb to thought, *only to suggest that the incarnation may (and most
certainly will) become not an expression of the spirit but a 'counter-spirit'*" (*Language as
Counter-Spirit*, pp. 3–4).

comparison with things, their archetypes" (*Prose Works,* II, 77).
Pre-Jungian archetypes were not especially numinous: in the
Guide to the Lakes a man on horseback is the archetype of his
reflection in the water beside the road (*Prose Works,* II, 192); in
the 1799 *Prelude,* stored-up mental images are said to have the
permanence of their archetypes, which are the natural scenes
from which they derive (i.283–87). It is clear that Wordsworth is
thinking in his customarily physical terms. If one has a word,
one should test it against a thought; if one has a thought, one
should test it against a thing—it is all really very satisfactory, a
sort of literary or critical equivalent of grasping at walls and
trees. By such standards the ultimate crime is that of Macpher-
son's *Ossian.* Claiming himself never to have been taken in by
this great opportunist pre-Romantic fake,[22] Wordsworth writes
in 1815: "From what I saw with my own eyes, I knew that the
imagery was spurious. In nature every thing is distinct, yet nothing defined into absolute independent singleness. In Macpher-
son's work, it is exactly the reverse; every thing (that is not stolen)
is in this manner defined, insulated, dislocated, deadened,—yet
nothing distinct. It will always be so," he adds, "when words are
substituted for things" (*Prose Works,* III, 77).[23]

[22]Which to judge from frequent borrowings in *The Vale of Esthwaite* was not
strictly true.

[23]It is a point that Wordsworth makes first when attacking Godwinian reason
in the fragment of an *Essay on Morals,* written in Germany at the end of 1798:
"The whole secret of this juggler's trick lies not in fitting words to things (which
would be a noble employment), but in fitting things to words" (*Prose Works,* I,
103). A particularly clear and interesting instance of the same distinction occurs
early in *Prelude,* Book VI, when the poet is musing on what went wrong for
Coleridge in his university career:

> I have thought
> Of thee, thy learning, gorgeous eloquence . . .
> Thy subtle speculations, toils abstruse
> Among the Schoolmen, and Platonic forms
> Of wild ideal pageantry, *shaped out*
> *From things well matched, or ill, and words for things—*
> The self-created sustenance of a mind
> Debarred from Nature's living images,
> Compelled to be a life unto itself . . .
> [*1805,* vi.305–14]

There is a very important distinction to be made between the substitution of words for things that takes place as the result of failure to connect them to their archetypes, and the tendency of words when being creatively used to achieve in their own right the status of things. In the first case words have become counters, and (at the risk of false etymology) the power they wield is a counter-spirit; in the second, they have become so enriched that they take on an imaginative life of their own. Wordsworth's defense of tautology in his 1800 note to *The Thorn* offers an insight into the very personal relationship with words that one sees being built up in his poetry. "Repetition and apparent tautology are frequent[ly] beauties of the highest kind," because "poetry is passion," and because words "ought to be weighed in the balance of feeling and not measured by the space which they occupy upon paper." "Among the chief of these reasons," Wordsworth concludes, "is the interest which the mind attaches to words, not only as symbols of the passion, but as *things,* active and efficient, which are themselves part of the passion. And further, from a spirit of fondness, exultation, and gratitude, the mind luxuriates in the repetition of words which appear successfully to communicate its feelings."[24]

As one might expect at the period of the Preface to *Lyrical Ballads,* Coleridge's thinking is in the background.[25] A matter of weeks before, Coleridge had written to Godwin: "I wish you to write a book on the power of words, and the processes by which human feelings form affinities with them." The processes as he

[24]*Lyrical Ballads,* ed. Brett and Jones, p. 289.

[25]Wordsworth was writing the Preface with the aid of Coleridge's notes, and for the moment it seemed to represent their joint views of poetry (*Collected Letters of Samuel Taylor Coleridge,* ed. Earl Leslie Griggs [6 vols.; Oxford, 1956–71], I, 627). It is difficult to know what to make of Wordsworth's repeated later claims that it had been written solely to please Coleridge, but it is not likely that he included any material without modifying it according to his own experience. With the addition of a second volume containing no Coleridge poems, and the disgraceful playing down of *The Ancient Mariner,* the collection had come to seem very much his own work; and whereas before it had been anonymous, it was now to appear with his name (alone) on the title page.

sees them are philosophical, or psychological—"Is *thinking* impossible without arbitrary signs? and how far is the word 'arbitrary' a misnomer?"[26]—but his final piece of advice is that Godwin should "endeavour to destroy the old antithesis of *words* and *things*, elevating, as it were, words into things, and living things too."[27] For Coleridge, words will be living things if it can be proven that their use is part of the organic process of human existence—"Are not words etc parts and germinations of the plant?"[28]—for Wordsworth they are so because their repetition brings out fondness, exultation, gratitude in the writer. Coleridge's thought is much more far-reaching. In effect he is positing the existence of an unconscious; whereas Wordsworth, characteristically taking over what he wants and leaving the rest on one side, is telling us how he values and feels the language of his own poetry.

Wordsworth's position appears limited beside Coleridge's speculation, and is certainly a long way from the thinking of the *Essay on Epitaphs*, in which language will take on a quite different autonomy and become at its best an incarnation of the thought. It may be, however, that he does not want to stray too far from his discussion of tautology and *The Thorn*. Already at this early period there are signs that he would like to make much larger claims. A group of four closely related fragments of blank verse belonging to summer 1799 is especially interesting in this respect.[29] The first three are concerned with the poet's failure to give form to his ideas, and may refer either to work on *The Recluse* or to inability to get going on the second part of the 1799 *Prelude*. The fourth presents this failure, very surprisingly for the period, as a relapse from full participation in the One life:

---

[26]*Collected Letters of Coleridge*, ed. Griggs, I, 625; Coleridge's italics.
[27]Ibid., p. 626.
[28]Ibid., p. 625.
[29]The fragments are entered by Wordsworth in fair copy on two facing pages of *Peter Bell* MS. 2 (Dove Cottage MS. 33), Norton *Prelude*, "MS. Drafts and Fragments," sec. 2, pp. 495-96.

> I seemed to learn
> That what we see of forms and images
> Which float along our minds, and what we feel
> Of active or recognizable thought,
> Prospectiveness, or intellect, or will,
> Not only is not worthy to be deemed
> Our being, to be prized as what we are,
> But is the very littleness of life.

"Such consciousness," Wordsworth continues, switching into the present tense to give still further emphasis,

> I deem but accidents,
> Relapses from the one interior life
> That lives in all things, sacred from the touch
> Of that false secondary power by which
> In weakness we create distinctions, then
> Believe that all our puny boundaries are things
> Which we perceive, and not which we have made—
> In which all beings live with God, themselves
> Are God, existing in one mighty whole,
> As undistinguishable as the cloudless east
> At noon is from the cloudless west, when all
> The hemisphere is one cerulean blue.

The passage is remarkable not only in taking up the extreme pantheist position that Spinoza and all his descendants down to Priestley, Coleridge, and Schelling seek desperately to avoid— "themselves / *Are* God"—but in its out-and-out rejection of the life of the mind. The internalized forms and images of Nature, which in *Tintern Abbey* had led through recollection to mystical experience, have come to seem mere littleness; the poet's intellectual life now appears to be a Urizenic fall into division, a creating of distinctions and categories in place of sharing in the totality of God.

The first of these extraordinary fragments had presented the poet's sense of failure no less powerfully, but in literary terms:

> nor had my voice
> Been silent—oftentimes had I burst forth
> In verse which with a strong and random light
> Touching an object in its prominent parts
> Created a memorial which to me
> Was all sufficient, and, to my own mind
> Recalling the whole picture, seemed to speak
> An universal language. Scattering thus
> In passion many a desultory sound,
> I deemed that I had adequately cloathed
> Meanings at which I hardly hinted, thoughts
> And forms of which I scarcely had produced
> A monument and arbitrary sign.

Again there is the failure to achieve universality, but this time it is a universal language. The poet's bursting forth in verse ought to have been the river of imagination; the strong yet random light is a sort of parody of the creative auxiliar light that comes from the mind to exercise its dominion over Nature;[30] the memorial stays merely personal; the passion can find no true embodiment.[31] If it were not that the mood is placed firmly in the past, it would be among the most despairing passages that Wordsworth ever wrote. As it is, it is the brief second fragment

[30]According to Hazlitt, in *The Spirit of the Age,* Wordsworth regarded himself as sharing with Rembrandt the ability to transform the world of common experience:

In the way in which that artist works something out of nothing, and transforms the stump of a tree, a common figure into an *ideal* object, by the gorgeous light and shade thrown upon it, he perceives an analogy to his own mode of investing the minute details of nature with an atmosphere of sentiment; and in pronouncing Rembrandt to be a man of genius, feels that he strengthens his own claim to the title. [*Complete Works of William Hazlitt,* ed. P. P. Howe (21 vols., 1930–34), XI, 93]

[31]Wordsworth for the moment accepts the conventional metaphor of language as the clothing of thought which he will later reject. In the light of Frances Ferguson's persuasive account of his epitaphic mode (*Language as Counter-Spirit,* chap. 5), it is difficult to know what to make of the seeming equation of "monument" and "arbitrary sign."

that is finally most impressive.[32] This time we are in the present;
the poet is referring to the patient, laborious act of composition,
describing what can be—perhaps indeed has been—achieved:

> In that considerate and laborious work,
> That patience which, admitting no neglect,
> [By] slow creation doth impart to speach
> Outline and substance, even till it has given
> A function kindred to organic power—
> The vital spirit of a perfect form.

Through the long-drawn-out creative process the writer imparts
to language (in effect, to his work) not just a circumscribing
outline, but also substance. Wordsworth's use of the word "function" is personal, and not always easy to define,[33] but the last two
all-important lines show the imparted substance as possessing a
power, essence, spirit, analogous to life itself—achieving, in the
poet's final paradox, a vital spirit, by virtue of the fact that it has
achieved a perfect form. The Romantic doctrine of organic
form, normally associated with Coleridge's Shakespeare lectures
of 1812 and his unacknowledged debt to Schlegel, had
seemingly been anticipated by Wordsworth as early as summer
1799.[34] Obviously it is tempting to think that Coleridge arrived

---

[32]The third fragment, with its account of "after-loathings, damps of discon-
tent / Returning ever like the obstinate pains / Of an uneasy spirit," is in fact
highly impressive too.

[33]Compare the "Conclusion" to the *Duddon Sonnets:*

> Still glides the stream, and shall for ever glide;
> The form remains, *the function never dies* . . .
>
> (xxxiii, 5–6)

and the lines quoted above from the *Essay on Epitaphs:* "those expressions which
are not what the garb is to the body, but what the body is to the soul, themselves *a
constituent part and power or function in the thought. . . .*" At *1805,* xii.378,
Wordsworth revises "The excellence, *pure spirit* and best power" to *1850* "pure
function."

[34]Coleridge's definition is found in fragmentary lecture notes published after
his death by his son-in-law. There is for once a passing reference to Schlegel ("a
continental critic"), as Coleridge begins his discussion of "the confounding
mechanical regularity with organic form":

at the idea earlier than has been assumed, and passed it on to Wordsworth when he and Dorothy came through Göttingen in April 1799. The case would then be exactly and conveniently parallel to the sudden appearance of the primary imagination in the account of the Infant Babe (*1799*, ii.267–310).[35] But whereas Coleridge becomes preoccupied with imagination, if not at once, at least quite soon after it appears in the 1799 *Prelude,* there is little evidence of his thinking in terms of organic form until the second course of Shakespeare lectures, thirteen years later.[36] It seems very possible that despite its resemblance to later positions, Wordsworth's thinking on this occasion is entirely his own, and should be taken to imply not a critical concept or viewpoint,

---

The form is mechanic when on any given material we impress a predetermined form, not necessarily arising out of the properties of the material, as when to a mass of wet clay we give whatever shape we wish it to retain when hardened. The organic form, on the other hand, is innate; it shapes as it develops itself from within, and the fulness of its development is one and the same with the perfection of its outward form. Such is the life, such is the form. [*Coleridge's Shakespearean Criticism,* ed. T. M. Raysor (2 vols., 1930), I, 224]

Schlegel's *Lectures* were published in Germany in 1809–10, and had been delivered in 1808. It is difficult to quarrel with Norman Fruman's account of this particular piece of plagiarism (*Coleridge, the Damaged Archangel* [London, 1972], pp. 141–61).

[35]For the circumstances of this appearance, see Jonathan Wordsworth, *The Borders of Vision* (Oxford, 1981), chap. 3. It could be argued that even before the publication of Schlegel's *Lectures,* Germany was a better place than England to hear discussion of organic form (or something like it). It is significant, for instance, that as Abrams points out, "German thought was much more receptive than English" to Young's *Conjectures on Original Composition* (1759), which makes persistent if unsystematic use of organic metaphor. "An *Original,*" Young writes, in a passage that clearly anticipates Romantic definitions, "may be said to be of a *vegetable* nature; it rises spontaneously from the vital root of genius; it *grows,* it is not *made.* Imitations are often a sort of *manufacture* wrought up by those *mechanics,* art and *labour,* out of pre-existent materials not their own" (M. H. Abrams, *The Mirror and the Lamp* [1953; reissued New York, 1971], p. 199).

[36]Organic metaphors are bound to crop up, of course. The letter to Godwin quoted above (pp. 58–59) goes so far as to regard individual words as "germinations of the plant" (*Collected Letters of Samuel Taylor Coleridge,* ed. Griggs, I, 625), but does not speculate as to the form of larger units. The assumption that Coleridge's first course of Shakespeare lectures in 1808, which preceded his reading of Schlegel, contained any reference to organic form is shown by Fruman (*Coleridge, the Damaged Archangel,* pp. 152 and 486–87) to have no solid basis.

but a wish that he may himself participate in the One Life through writing that has achieved a universal, and therefore an organic, language. If Coleridge's influence is present at all, perhaps instead of looking forward to the period of his critical lectures, one should look back to the time when speculation of every kind had seemed to find energy and support in a pantheist life force:

> And what if all of animated nature
> Be but organic harps diversely framed,
> That tremble into thought as o'er them sweeps
> Plastic and vast, one intellectual breeze,
> At once the soul of each, and God of all?
> [*Eolian Harp*, ll. 44-48]

As a representative of animated nature, the poet trembles into thought; as a creator in his own right, he imparts to his work

> A function kindred to organic power—
> The vital spirit of a perfect form.

In practice the life that Wordsworth gave, or hoped to give, in his poetry was a storing up—a making permanent, and making available—of impressions:

> and I would give
> While yet we may, as far as words can give,
> A substance and a life to what I feel:
> I would enshrine the spirit of the past
> For future restoration.
> [*1805*, xi.338-42]

The emotions of the moment, often themselves deriving from the past, are to be treasured in a "casket of immortal verse," for the sake of the poet himself, and for the sake of those that follow. The wish that feeling may have the permanence of the natural forms with which it is associated leads in the Preface to

Lyrical Ballads to a quest for language that shall have a corresponding permanence. At one moment Wordsworth goes so far as to claim that "the *best* part of language is originally derived" from objects with which the peasant is in contact.[37] Coleridge's derision in *Biographia Literaria* is well known and to the point, but as in his commentary on the "seer blest" of *Intimations*, he ignores what is taking place beneath the overstatement.[38] The child is a symbol, not a prodigy; and language at its purest is felt to derive from natural objects, not because the poet is unaware of the limits of a peasant's vocabulary, but because he associates such objects with the sources of his own power and wish to communicate. Within the mind they have established their permanence: they are the "forms of beauty" that in *Tintern Abbey* "have not been . . ./ As is a landscape to a blind man's eye" (ll.23-25), the forms that in Part I of the 1799 *Prelude*

> exist with independent life,
> And, like their archetypes, know no decay.
> [*1799*, i.285-87]

Whether the images are knowingly and pleasurably "fastened" upon the brain (*Pedlar*, ll.39-41), or stamped upon it through painful experience (the "spots of time"; *1799*, i.258-374), or merely left there as unconscious, "collateral" impressions (*1799*, i.418-26), they are already a kind of language, a silent poetry of the mind that recalls emotion and experience to which only words can give an outward life. Wordsworth was no doubt aware of replacing Hartley's millenarian associationism with his own more personal brand:

---

[37] *Lyrical Ballads*, ed. Brett and Jones, p. 245.

[38] For Coleridge's scathing remarks on rustics and "the best part of language," see *Biographia Literaria*, ed. George Watson (London and New York, 1956; corrected ed., 1965), pp. 197-98. For his surely deliberate obtuseness over the child of *Intimations*, see *Biographia Literaria*, p. 260: "Children at this age give us no such information of themselves; at what time were we dipt in the Lethe, which has produced such utter oblivion of a state so godlike?"

                              The earth
And common face of Nature spake to me
Rememberable things—sometimes, 'tis true,
By quaint associations, yet not vain
Nor profitless, if haply they impressed
Collateral objects and appearances,
Albeit lifeless then, and doomed to sleep
Until maturer seasons called them forth
To impregnate and to elevate the mind.
                              [*1799*, i.418-26]

Rememberable things do not have to be remembered—they
have to be linked by associations, however quaint, that will later
call them back to a mind that can give them their true
Wordsworthian value. In a magnificent phrase, the child's immediate joy "Wearied itself out of the memory," but

     The scenes which were a witness of that joy
     Remained, in their substantial lineaments
     Depicted on the brain, and to the eye
     Were visible, a daily sight.
                              [*1799*, i.427-32]

It is of course to the inward eye—the eye that will come to seem
"the bliss of solitude"—that the scenes are daily visible. In bringing them repeatedly to mind, the poet revisits and revalues past
emotions "purifying thus / The elements of feeling and of
thought" (*1799*, i.137-38), and preserving for the future that
which could not originally have been known to be precious:

                         And thus
     By the impressive agency of fear,
     By pleasure and repeated happiness—
     So frequently repeated—and by force
     Of obscure feelings representative
     Of joys that were forgotten, these same scenes,
     So beauteous and majestic in themselves,
     Though yet the day was distant, did at length

Become habitually dear, and all
Their hues and forms were by invisible links
Allied to the affections.

[*1799*, i.432-42]

In the "obscure feelings representative / Of joys that were forgotten" lie not just the sources of adult confidence, but the
"obscure sense / Of possible sublimity" that is the poet's inspiration as he writes.[39] Whether or not associationism can be in
general a force for good, there is no reason to doubt that in the
development of Wordsworth's own mind—and in the poetry
that records that development—it is extremely important. It is in
such a context that one should read the strange, at first sight
largely incomprehensible, sequence from the end of *Prelude*,
Book V, that was quoted at the beginning of this paper:

> Visionary power
> Attends upon the motions of the winds
> Embodied in the mystery of words;
> There darkness makes abode, and all the host
> Of shadowy things do work their changes there
> As in a mansion like their proper home.
> Even forms and substances are circumfused
> By that transparent veil with light divine,
> And through the turnings intricate of verse

---

[39]   I deem not profitless these fleeting moods
Of shadowy exaltation; not for this,
That they are kindred to our purer mind
And intellectual life, but that the soul—
Remembering how she felt, but what she felt
Remembering not—retains an obscure sense
Of possible sublimity, to which
With growing faculties she doth aspire,
With faculties still growing, feeling still
That whatsoever point they gain they still
Have something to pursue.

(From the fragment "In storm and tempest," incorporated in *The Prelude* as
1799, ii.358-73, but actually written at Alfoxden a year earlier than the poet's
reference to "obscure feelings representative" in *1799*, i.435-37. The opening
lines of the passage are quoted below, p. 68.)

Present themselves as objects recognized
In flashes, and with a glory scarce their own.
[*1805*, v.619-29]

On a superficial level the passage shows Wordsworth in March
1804 trying to excuse himself for not having succeeded in writing a book about "Books." He has just alleged, not very convincingly, that those who have been brought up in the country get a
special pleasure from what he terms "the great Nature that exists
in works / Of mighty poets"—hence apparently his reference to
"the motions of the winds / Embodied in the mystery of words."
But this train of thought hardly seems to explain the preoccupations of the poetry. How much effect are the winds really felt to
have in Wordsworth's sentence? Where is it that the enigmatic
"darkness makes abode"—in winds? or in words? What would be
the difference if one left the winds out, and read: "Visionary
power / Attends upon . . . the mystery of words"? A great deal
falls into place if one realizes that the mighty poet whom
Wordsworth has in mind is not Shakespeare, or Milton, or even
the Coleridge of *The Eolian Harp,* but his own earlier self. A
cluster of verbal echoes refers us back to Alfoxden, and what
may well be the earliest lines in *The Prelude:*

> and I would stand
> Beneath some rock, listening to sounds that are
> The ghostly language of the ancient earth,
> Or make their dim abode in distant winds.
> Thence did I drink the visionary power.[40]
> [*1799*, ii.356-60/*1805*, ii.326-30]

The Wordsworth of Book V is looking back to spring 1798 as the
period at which it had seemed possible to perceive directly the
transcendental forces of Nature. But his concern now is with

[40]For the remainder of the passage, see note 39, above. The lines were written
in the third person in early February 1798 and incorporated in *The Prelude* in
autumn 1799.

language—not the unarticulated "sounds that are / The ghostly language of the ancient earth," but the mystery of words in which he had been able to embody his response. In effect he is saying: Visionary power is inherent in the language I then used. The reassuring corollary is to be found in lines written a day or two later, which link the first of the "spots of time" to the later period of happiness, as he wandered with Mary Hutchinson and Dorothy "in daily presence of... the naked pool and dreary crags / And... melancholy beacon" that had been the "involutes"[41] of his early traumatic experience:

> so feeling comes in aid
> Of feeling, and diversity of strength
> Attends us, if but once we have been strong.
> [*1805*, xi.325-27]

Wordsworth is seen drawing strength from his own inspired earlier poetry in very much the same way that he draws it from memories of an imaginative childhood. The phrase "There darkness makes abode" comes to be a reference to the "obscure sense / Of possible sublimity" with which the earlier experience had left him. At the same time it is the expression of a new hope that in the uncomprehended workings of language itself there are creative powers. The "darkness" in which the host of shadowy things are working their changes is the first cousin of the "greatness" that will similarly "make abode" in the much more famous piece of verse that was written a few weeks later directly about imagination:

---

[41]The term is De Quincey's: "I have been struck," he writes in *Suspiria de Profundis*, "with the important truth that far more of our deepest thoughts and feelings pass to us through perplexed combinations of *concrete* objects, pass to us as *involutes* (if I may coin that word) in compound experiences incapable of being disentangled, than ever reach us directly and in their own abstract shapes" (*Collected Writings of Thomas de Quincey*, ed. Masson, I, 39). The "spots of time" (in their original position in Part I of the 1799 *Prelude*) are discussed at some length, and related to De Quincey's insight, in chap. 2 of *The Borders of Vision*.

> I was lost as in a cloud,
> Halted without a struggle to break through,
> And now, recovering, to my soul I say
> 'I recognize thy glory'. In such strength
> Of usurpation, in such visitings
> Of awful promise, when the light of sense
> Goes out in flashes that have shewn to us
> The invisible world, doth greatness make abode . . .
>
> [*1805*, vi.529–36]

The cloud that halts the mental traveler in these lines from Book VI is specifically the "unfathered vapour" of imagination. It is, one feels, far better understood by the poet himself, as well as far more impressive, than the darkness of the earlier passage. Yet this darkness has very positive properties. It leads as in the later sequence to flashes of recognition, but en route has been described much less predictably as a veil. In Book IV—

> Gently did my soul
> Put off her veil, and, self-transmuted, stood
> Naked as in the presence of her God
>
> [iv.140–42]

—he had used the traditional veil that closes off perception, preserving decencies and distance; but here the veil is an active force that circumfuses the external world of forms and substances with light divine—"apparels" them "with celestial light," adds to them "The light that never was, on sea or land" (*Peele Castle*, l.15).[42] Wordsworth is writing about the making of poetry, and it might be convenient to think of the darkness of Book V as defining the secondary, or poetic, imagination, so as to prepare the way for definition of the primary in Book VI. It isn't so. Both passages deal with the primary, but in the earlier it

---

[42] In Coleridge's terms, which Wordsworth must surely have in mind, the veil is "A light, a glory, and a luminous cloud / Enveloping the earth" (*Letter to Sara Hutchinson*, ll.303–4).

is seen in the workings of language. Like Coleridge's secret ministry of frost, or the sea of mist on Snowdon, language is for Wordsworth a silent transforming power. Veiled (in the conventional sense) behind the lines of Book V is the hope that neither he nor Coleridge ever dared to express, that poetry itself, the act of writing, is "a repetition in the finite mind of the eternal act of creation in the infinite I AM"—a repetition that does not always, or merely, "co-exist with the conscious will."[43] It is for this reason that the correspondent breeze of the Preamble becomes incarnate in the mystery of words, and for this reason that one hears so many echoes from Book V when Wordsworth comes to define the "visitings of awful promise," and that very special hope that consists of

> Effort, and expectation, and desire,
> And something evermore about to be.
> [*1805*, vi.541-42]

No wonder that language out of control should appear to vitiate and dissolve (where the imagination struggles at all events to idealize and to unify), and that Wordsworth should think it able, if rightly and creatively used, to "uphold, and feed, and leave in quiet, like the power of gravitation, or the air we breathe." At its best Wordsworth's prose can be as rich in associations as his verse—as full of shadowy things that are working their changes in the darkness of the language. "Uphold" is certainly a word that he repeats "from a spirit of fondness, exultation, and gratitude," and which is felt to have its own especial resonance, partly acquired through this repetition, partly innate. In *Prelude*, Book X, Nature and human love have *upheld* the poet in his hour of crisis, and *uphold* him still at the time of writing (*1805*, x.921-29). In a most untypical passage of Book III we hear of

---

[43]Coleridge, *Biographia Literaria*, ed. Watson, p. 167.

> visitings
> Of the *upholder*, of the tranquil soul,
> Which underneath all passion lives secure
> A steadfast life.
>
> [*1805*, iii.115–18]

Margaret in *The Ruined Cottage* had "*upheld* the cool refreshment, drawn" from a well that came to symbolize outgoing love and the brotherhood of Nature and man (ll.98–103). Then there are "those first affections" of the Ode,

> Those shadowy recollections
> Which be they what they may
> Are yet the fountain light of all our day
> Are yet the master light of all our seeing
> *Uphold* us cherish us and make
> Our noisy years seem moments in the being
> Of the eternal silence . . .[44]

And, among many further instances, there is Wordsworth's confident description in *1805*, Book XII, of poets as "Men . . . of other mold,"

> Who are *their own upholders*, to themselves
> Encouragement, and energy, and will,
> Expressing liveliest thoughts in lively words
> As native passion dictates.
>
> [*1805*, xii.260–64]

These men who are "their own upholders" have surely achieved a Wordsworthian ideal. They have a power that is self-sufficing and self-supporting; they are "blest in thoughts / That are their own perfection and reward" (*1805*, vi.545–46), and they are capable of transforming these thoughts into poetry that is the natural incarnation of their passion. And yet for all their

---

[44]*Intimations*, ll. 147–53, in the text of 1804 (Jared R. Curtis, *Wordsworth's Experiments with Tradition* [Ithaca and London, 1971], pp. 164–70).

qualities and attainments, and despite the fact that this is the group to which Wordsworth himself belongs, one should expect to find them taking a second place. "Others, too, / There are among the walks of homely life," the passage continues, "*Still higher*":

> Theirs is the language of the heavens, the power,
> The thought, the image, and the silent joy;
> Words are but under-agents in their souls—
> When they are grasping with their greatest strength
> They do not breathe among them.
>
> [*1805*, xii.270-74]

To speak on earth the language of the heavens is indeed "to make / Our noisy years seem moments in the being / Of the eternal silence." For poets in general, words are "external things" that may at any time assume dominion over thoughts: in silent poets, language is a function of the soul. The prefix "under" ("Words are but *under*-agents") works in various ways. It implies, of course, the unimportance of words as such, for those who speak the language of the heavens; but it suggests while doing so that the silent poet is peculiarly in touch with Wordsworthian sources of power—the "under-soul" that is "hushed" as imagination sleeps at Cambridge (*1805*, iii.539-40), the "under-presence" of Snowdon that is "The sense of God, or whatso'er is dim / Or vast in its own being" (*1805*, xiii.71-73). When grasping with their greatest strength—the physicality of Wordsworth's metaphor has more than usual appropriateness—silent poets have transcended not just ordinary speech but the liveliest embodiments of native passion. They are fully perceptive; and fully creative too, in so far as perception *is* creation. John Wordsworth, the original silent poet, brings "from the solitude / Of the vast sea" "an eye practiced like a blind man's touch" (*When to the attractions of the busy world*, ll.80-83); and a similar perceptiveness heightened into creativity can be brought out in the shepherd Michael, who is his counterpart on land.[45] Such men have the spontaneity that the vocal poet could have if mind could print upon mind, if it were possible to inscribe as with the silence of the thought. But even when words are truly an incarnation, the creative process implies in practice a standing back.[46] In effect the silent poet is a child who can prolong the state of innocence because he does not have responsibilities—or has them only within a limited sphere. Wordsworth as a teacher has accepted the obligation to communicate; however envious he may be, he is bound to the tools of his trade. If his work is truly to become "A power like one of Nature's" (*1805*, xii.312), he must find the colors and words hitherto unknown to man—a barrier must be broken down, a border crossed. "Is there not," he asks poignantly in *Home at Grasmere,* at a moment when things are not going too well,

[45]Among the unused drafts of *Michael* in Dove Cottage MS. 30 there is a touching scene in which the peasant reveals "sudden recognitions, that were like / Creations in the mind, and were indeed / Creations often." "Then," Wordsworth continues,

> when he discoursed
> Of mountain sights, this untaught shepherd stood
> Before the man with whom he so conversed,
> And looked at him as with a poet's eye.

(*Poetical Works of William Wordsworth,* ed. Ernest de Selincourt and Helen Darbishire [5 vols.; Oxford, 1940–49], II, 482.)
[46]At times, of course, the active poet will choose to evoke the silent poetry of the mind that is merely the halfway stage in a fully creative process. Wordsworth does so beautifully in the *Michael* drafts, again using the image of the blind man's special sensitivity:

> If, looking round, I have perchance perceived
> Some vestiges of human hands, some stir
> Of human passion, they to me are sweet
> As lightest sunbreak, or the sudden sound
> Of music to a blind man's ear who sits
> Alone and silent in the summer shade.
> [*Oxford Wordsworth*, II, 480]

An art, a music, and a stream of words
That shall be life, the acknowledged voice of life?[47]

"Language if it do not uphold, and feed, and leave in quiet, like the power of gravitation, or the air we breathe"—perhaps one hardly needs to go on with the game of associations, but it cannot fail to be significant that the single place in Wordsworth's poetry where the word "gravitation" appears is the *Prelude* account of the Infant Babe and the origins of imagination in the love of a mother for her child:

> [In] this beloved presence there exists
> A virtue which irradiates and exalts
> All objects through all intercourse of sense.
> No outcast *he*...

(Unlike the adult poet; and unlike Wordsworth the child after the early death of his mother.)

> No outcast he, bewildered and depressed;
> Along his infant veins are interfused
> The *gravitation* and the filial bond
> Of Nature that connect him with the world.
>   [*1799*, ii.288-94]

Such for Wordsworth is the power and function of language. It is a primal reassurance of belonging, a connection with the world that is at the same time a source and guarantee of adult vision. In its highest form it is imagination itself, the corresponding internal energy of the *Essay Supplementary* that coincides with, and balances, the external correspondent breeze. If only it

[47]*Home at Grasmere*, ed. Beth Darlington (Ithaca, 1977), p. 76, ll.621-22. To put it all in Coleridge's more theoretical, more pompous terms, words must become "symbols, harmonious in themselves, and consubstantial with the truths, of which they are the *conductors*" (*Lay Sermons*, ed. R. J. White [London and Princeton, 1972], p. 29; Coleridge's italics).

could be inscribed as with the silence of the thought—if mind could stamp its image upon mind as in the days when the poet himself had "held mute dialogues with his mother's heart," and possessed as of right the "virtue which irradiates . . . / All objects through all intercourse of sense."

PART II
THE ACHIEVEMENT
OF M. H. ABRAMS

History as Metaphor:
Or, Is M. H. Abrams a Mirror, or
a Lamp, or a Fountain, or . . . ?

WAYNE C. BOOTH

In recent years, M. H. Abrams has speculated a good deal about what we know and how we know it, and as we honor his historical and critical achievement it is surely appropriate to begin with that kind of question. What do we *know* about him and his work? How does what we know apply to questions about the cognitive value of literary history? Influenced by certain modern philosophers, everyone these days seems to divide our knowing into "knowing how" and "knowing that." We certainly do not *know how* Abrams does his literary histories; he has himself confessed not only that before he does them he doesn't yet know how to, but also that after they are done he cannot tell us how he or anyone else should set about to do another one.[1] We are not entirely clear even about our knowledge *that* it was done. To know that a thing is depends finally on our having some sense of *what* it is, and one need not read very far in comments

[1] M. H. Abrams, "Rationality and Imagination in Cultural History: A Reply to Wayne Booth," *Critical Inquiry,* 2 (Spring 1976), 447–64, esp. 447–48; reprinted in my *Critical Understanding: The Powers and Limits of Pluralism* (Chicago, 1979), pp. 175–94. Hereafter referred to as *CI* and *CU.*

WAYNE C. BOOTH

on *The Mirror and the Lamp* and *Natural Supernaturalism* to discover immense disagreement about precisely what such things
are. I am not thinking of superficial disagreements about
terminology—are they literary history, cultural history, literary
theory, literary criticism, history of ideas, or what not?—but of
more troublesome questions about the kind of knowledge they
give us, if any. I propose today to honor those two curiously
elusive works by at least complicating, if not finally clarifying,
our notions of what they are.

My subject is of course only partially M. H. Abrams. I take him
as a representative of the problems raised when we throw together questions about the "natures" of three vexed topics:
metaphor, literary history, and truth or validity. He is representative in two senses. We wouldn't be here today if many of us did
not see him as representing the best we know in literary history.
To me Abrams is the best historian of ideas, as ideas relate to
literature and literary criticism, that the world has known—
though I am willing to qualify the judgment slightly by confess-
ing that there might be one or two others I have not read. On
the other hand, Abrams is representative of the problems raised
when a historian not only traces prominent metaphorical views
of the world but accounts for their history in an inherently
metaphorical language of his own. If Abrams merely described
how others have talked of poets as mirrors and lamps, or of ideas
spiraling down through millennia, our subject would be somewhat different (though I must confess that to imagine him doing
so is as hard as imagining those entirely implausible "other possible worlds" that philosophers play with these days). But his
own language for what he is doing goes far beyond the simple
"mirroring" of historical truth that most historians implicitly
claim for themselves. Professing a pluralism that he finds best
described with metaphors of perspectivism,[2] claiming to write a
book, *Natural Supernaturalism,* that in its spiral form is itself

²*CI*, pp. 459–60, *CU*, pp. 189–90.

iconic of the path traced in history by the ideas it faithfully mirrors,[3] Abrams does not make things easy for us when we ask what he is doing, really, and how his work relates to other possible histories of the same events.

Whether metaphors can carry any truth, or any novel truth, is a question that everyone seems to be debating these days.[4] We may, like Abrams himself, choose to assume that metaphorical narratives somehow or other teach us something; we may assume, as I do, that his spiral tracing of the way ideas of a spiraling history themselves spiraled through modern history offers cognitive rewards along with its immense value as historical entertainment. But to make that assumption, in the teeth of many a professional philosopher, is to raise once again the "know what" question. What kind of teaching is this? I can here hope only to make a start on that question, by trying to understand what kind of teaching Abrams implicitly claims for himself.

We could easily be led astray if we took straight his many claims to literal reporting. It is of course true that he works unusually hard to give a just account of what his various subjects actually wrote, and he is properly offended when anyone suggests that historians need not, indeed cannot, understand the documents they read or give an accurate report on the reading.[5] The question is whether, if we grant a privileged cognitive status to the historian who works in Abrams' way, we are at the same time granting that the resulting history is literal and not metaphorical. Obviously our answer depends on what we mean

[3] *CI*, pp. 449-50; *CU*, pp. 178-79.
[4] The startling spread of the debate can be realized only by looking at recent bibliographies, beginning, perhaps, with Shibles' immense compendium, *Metaphor: An Annotated Bibliography and History* (Whitewater, Wis., 1971). A nicely confusing start on the semantic ambiguities underlying every term in the debate can be made by reading *On Metaphor*, ed. Sheldon Sacks (Chicago, 1979), most of which appeared originally as a special issue of *Critical Inquiry*, 5 (Autumn 1978). The most striking contrast with what I shall be saying here is provided by Donald Davidson's essay "What Metaphors Mean," pp. 31-47.
[5] See especially his "The Deconstructive Angel," *Critical Inquiry*, 3 (Spring 1977), 425-38. See also *CI*, pp. 455-58; *CU*, pp. 184-88.

[8 1]

by metaphor, but I think that Abrams can be shown to be a metaphorist according to any standard definition.

The easy way would be to accept the increasingly popular view that everything not strictly literal is metaphoric. In that view, which provides us with a useful general term, metaphor, for all figures of speech that are not ironic, metonymy becomes one kind of metaphor, because a reduced part is made to stand for a whole. All histories are by nature metonymic, their stories made to stand for wholes that are immeasurably more complex. Except for strictly literal transcripts that "mirror" every word, any report, any outline, any summary, and *a fortiori* any tracing of connections among summarized statements reduces texts and sequences into something they were not. Metonymy! Therefore metaphor! In short, even when dealing with individual texts, even when meaning to mirror what he considers their "determinate" meanings, Abrams is at best an inverted telescope employing intricate filters that eliminate details, deliberately or accidentally.

If even the best intellectual reporting of individual texts entails the metonymy of the skeleton-taken-for-the-whole, how much more obviously metaphorical—in the same very broad sense of the word—is every account that tries to make historical sense of an event or period or sequence of either. Because of the inherent complexities of all human events, the potential list of causes for any one event, even the simplest, is indeterminately large. Events as complex as what we call Romanticism, or the life of Wordsworth, or the making of any one of his poems offer an even more strikingly abundant number of handles for the historian. Unless he decides to give us mere chronicle—"and *then* Wordsworth wrote some lyrical ballads and a preface to a volume of that name, and *then* he revised that preface, and *meanwhile* he was planning and beginning to write a trilogy"—he will be choosing a limited number of causal or temporal patterns from an indeterminately large list of possibilities. Indeed, even the chronicler of mere temporal sequence is choosing, more or less unwittingly, a set of causes that are privileged by the prevailing notions of his time. As our brethren from overseas insist, it is not, as we may have thought, self-evident that the expression "And then Wordsworth wrote *Tintern Abbey*" is literal, in contrast with statements about other causes less "proximate" or "sufficient." What "really" wrote *Tintern Abbey* was, one might say, the institution of writing realizing itself in his time; or class and culture clashing in the mind and heart of the middle class. Though we may want to preserve a privileged status for the author as composing cause, we can no longer maintain, as I once thought, that the privilege is conferred by the superior literalness of such talk.

But we need not depend on an imperialist expansion of what "metaphor" means to consider Abrams as essentially metaphorical. He himself steadily reminds us of it in at least two ways. There is first the simple and inescapable fact that even when Abrams is aspiring most diligently to give a literal report, he cannot escape metaphorical language—and here I retreat to a more conventional and I think more useful definition, derived from the classical rhetoricians: metaphor as an "abnormal" joining of two conceptual domains, a joining that twists our normal ways of separating those domains. Defining figures of speech in terms of normality in this way has always given trouble, because what is normal shifts from day to day; live metaphors quickly sicken into cliché and soon perish. If Abrams does not strike us as a highly metaphorical writer, it is only because most of his metaphors are deceptively close to the normal—that is to say, they have *almost* an air of literalness about them: "As the *fruit* of a century's endeavors, then, Kant formulates the view ..."; "In this characteristic document of romantic philosophy in Germany, the extraordinary importance attributed to aesthetic invention may be regarded as the *climax* of a general *tendency* ..."; "In Jean Paul's *Orphic ejaculations* on the nature of genius, ... we can *dimly make out* some familiar *traits*" (*The Mirror and the Lamp*, pp. 208-11). One finds many such metaphors on every page of every literary history. If I try to imagine what a fully literal statement—that is, a fully "normal" way of talking about causation—might be, I soon am staggered with the immense burden of metaphor that is carried by even our most careful thought about such matters—that is to say, by the thought of M. H. Abrams.

II

Before looking more closely at how this metaphorist works, we should understand why the problem of metaphor is more acute when we consider his work than it would be if we were considering certain "histories" that are more aggressively metaphorical, such as *The Greening of America* or Norman Mailer's *Why Are We in Viet Nam?* The answer surely lies in Abrams' repeated and justified claims to being sound, right, solid. When a metaphorist is either careless or openly playful with his metaphors, we know how to discount the color and appraise the core of truth, if there is one. Or at least we think we do. But when a metaphorist self-evidently cares about being sound, sound not only in his choice and interpretation of data but in his metaphorical organization of the data, we meet a special kind of challenge. Our response to his metaphorical organization is largely the same one we make when we offer to judge the truth or validity of any particular metaphor: Say something to me that is not only new—that's too easy—but also important because sound.

It could be argued that every history that teaches us something important depends on persuading us that a novel metaphor is sound. No historian ever impresses us for long simply by accumulating or correcting data; soundness of data is important, obviously, but the historians who endure for us show a surprising invulnerability to corrections of their data. They survive precisely because their brief accounts—and, as my talk of metonymy suggests, all histories are in one sense shockingly brief—seem to some degree adequate to the immense unknown heaps of data from which their story has been abstracted. In short, their inevitable reductions impress us as genuinely *abstracted*, not merely invented. Those that make the strongest claims to literal accuracy, and thus risk most our objections about omission, succeed only if they persuade us that what they give does in fact stand for the whole. They can do that only if they can offer some metaphor that combines the data explicitly offered into a picture that credibly includes the mountains of data that must be excluded. They usually dramatize their quality as metonymic narrative by explicit reference to risings or fallings, *Aufstiege* or *Untergänge*, circlings or spiralings. Like all metaphors, they put things together in a new way, but by calling themselves histories they make a more blatant claim to cognitive assent than our usual metaphors: "I am not just illuminating, I am true."

Thus metaphoric novelty and claims to truth are somehow fused, in all history that we care about. The historian has managed to be original, as we say, by telling a story that nobody else has told before, and telling it in a way that will make everyone agree that the narrative, though obviously metaphorical in this special sense, *ought* to be told this way, that it is in some sense true, though necessarily reductive.

Whether fulfilling the claim to truth (or "referentiality") is tough or easy will depend in part on what we mean by "true." We might decide, for example, to fill the time here with statements that are factually accurate. I think I could fill forty minutes of your time with mostly accurate statements about Abrams. But the only ones I could count on everyone's accepting would be what we call factual, and though some of us might be willing to use the word truth for such sound stuff, all of us would by the end be ready to storm the Bastille in the name of—well, surely not of what is *un*sound. But of what, then? Of something interesting, surely, and that means something novel, and that in turn means something that puts a great number of things together as nobody has ever put them before: in short, it means making a metaphoric object that seems to require a fancier term than metaphor—macrometaphor, perhaps, or "grand metaphor."

Novelty by itself is even more easily achieved than dull soundness. Roland Barthes, a sophisticated master of juicy surprises, has neatly formulated the procedure for making novelties if, unlike Abrams, we no longer worry about soundness. The instructions are found in a witty paragraph labeled "*En fait,*" in his autobiographic contribution to the series *Écrivains de toujours.*[6]

"So you believe that the purpose of catch-as-catch-can wrestling is to win? Not at all, it is to gain understanding.... You have the notion that drama is fictional, idealized, by comparison with life? Not at all ... [the truth is just the reverse]. Gangster movies are not highly emotional, as people have thought, but intellectual. So you see Jules Verne as a writer of travel adventures? Of course he is not; rather he writes about stuffy constraints." Such paradoxical twists are in unlimited supply, he goes on, and they are provided by a simple logical operator, the expression "in fact": "Strip tease is not at all an erotic solicitation; in fact it strips womankind of all sex." And so on. The very mention of such easy and automatic inversions, even when surrounded with Barthes' immensely complex ironies, serves nicely as contrast with the kind of claim Abrams himself would want to make about his efforts to transform received opinions about the past.

There may seem to be just a breath of Barthes' automatic manufacture of paradox in my title, which for completeness should have been, "Is M. H. Abrams a mirror, a lamp, or a fountain? An instrument? A poet, perhaps—that is, a maker, a creator? A rung on the ladder of historical progress? Or a giant stride in cultural history?" You had thought that M. H. Abrams was quite literally a historian of literature and criticism? Well, in fact—*in fact* he can be described adequately only in metaphors,

---

[6]*Roland Barthes par Roland Barthes* (Paris, 1975), p. 86.

as a metaphorical critic of metaphor, something that even he has never deigned to admit. But if that is so, how do we appraise the soundness of his metaphors or of the metaphors we apply to him?

Abrams has insisted both that intellectual and creative movements come in many shapes and shades and that at least some of them are better described with metaphor than with literal terms. It is not just that views of poetry, and thus of kinds of criticism, are inherently many—views expressive, rhetorical, mimetic, and objective. It is that both Abrams and those critics and philosophers whose history he traces insist on metaphor: the poet is a lamp, a fountain, a mirror, an instrument, a sculptor, or what not. And once he rises—or sinks—into metaphor, the problem of saying not just what is novel but also sound and important becomes acute indeed. Is M. H. Abrams as historian and critical pluralist to be thought of as, say, a bottle opener? No? Well, then, how about as doorkeeper of a house of ill repute who has been ordered to accept all comers? A manufacturer of kaleidoscopes? A Waring blender? A computer program with a nearly infinite data capacity? These metaphors are all obviously inappropriate, but they all are true in some sense—he opens what was closed, he accepts all or nearly all comers, he multiplies perspectives, he produces new blendings of what had been thought distinct, he processes immensely complex data. Something is plainly "off" in each of these metaphors, but how do we argue such claims?

III

As I have said, Abrams refuses to give much explicit help in such matters. He is extraordinarily free and easy in tracing what poets and critics and philosophers have said, and then in lumping them under general metaphors derived mainly from their own words. But he is reticent, even when pushed, about what *he* is as he does the tracing.

Suppose we extract his implicit claims for himself, using his own schema from *The Mirror and the Lamp:*

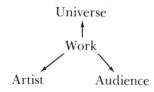

Abrams, you will remember, labels theories of poetry that center on the artist as "expressive," theories relating the work to the universe as "mimetic," theories working along the vector between work and audience as "pragmatic," and theories that deal with "the work itself" as "objective." Presumably theories of what Abrams himself does might fall somewhere on the same chart.

The Mirror

Perhaps most obviously there is a strong element of *mirror* talk in most of his self-descriptions. It is quite clear, throughout both of his histories, that he sees himself as *referring to* or *reflecting* something that is in the record, not something that he merely spins out of his own imaginings or preferences. Indeed, he is not only a mirror: his aspiration is to be a particularly well-polished mirror, introducing so little distortion that one might expect him to feel slightly violated by my talking of his projects as metaphorical at all. Often he sounds as if he thought of himself as the most literal-minded of reporters, without even the freedoms that the older mimetic critics always gave to poets when they described them as holding a mirror up to nature. Abrams is not, after all, a mirror held up to nature; he is a mirror held up to human statements that are informed by determinate human intentions. These texts not only happened; they were intended, and he reports the real intentions, or tries to.

Though the texts can be interpreted in many ways, he claims finally that his history is, like William James's *Principles of Psy-*

chology, forged "in the teeth of irreducible and stubborn facts."[7] And his facts are the meanings that are really in the texts: the authors he treats, he says, wrote "in order to be understood," their sentences were "designed" to have a core of determinate meanings.

Poems, too, he sees as having at least a core of determinate meanings available to all competent readers. Such readers are presumably allowed to be lamps in only a very limited sense: they can provide a light on the text that will enable *their* readers to see what *is there.* But they are not to be colored strobe lights, let alone fountains spewing forth new realities, or poets imitating the creative act of God by bringing new realities into the world. Whatever they do is finally in the service of mirroring, and such mirroring is, it seems, not essentially resistant to a literal account: his history is largely of "literal" causes and relations found in what "literally" happened. In his recent statements about pluralism, he is eager to defend himself as in pursuit of causes that he considers quite literal: "when I do point to parallels and analogues, they are meant to be explicable, in part, by the persistent and subtle play of literal causes, or interinfluences." When he traces the "assimilation of the right-angled biblical patterns of Paradise–Fall–Redemption–Paradise Regained into the post-biblical circular pattern of Unity–Multiplicity–Unity Regained," the tracing, he says, is not simply assertion by analogy; the shift is shown to be the "product of explicit interpretations of biblical history." "And the Romantic adaptation of this pattern of history . . . is shown . . . to be the product of . . . writers . . . who, entirely explicitly, set out to translate the truth." What he traces is what was "the deliberate and specifically formulated" enterprises of the authors he discusses.[8]

In short, it is made to sound as literal as literal could be. The

---

[7]*CI,* p. 455; *CU,* p. 184.
[8]*CI,* pp. 453–54; *CU,* pp. 182–83.

historian's act is thus describable, without metaphor, as reporting on a historical reality. If we choose to call that act mirroring or reflecting, that is our choice and not, seemingly, Abrams'. Yet he has forced us into metaphor, and as we shall see, he himself has other optical instruments in mind.

The Instrument and the Sculptor

To do justice to his chart, we must next take seriously, if only for a moment, the ways in which his talk about himself suggests two metaphors often placed in polar opposition in traditional aesthetic debate: the poem (or history) as "pragmatic" instrument and the poem (or history) as pure art, to be considered "objectively" for its formal beauty. Neither of these possibilities is initially quite as plausible, applied to Abrams, as the notion of accurate reflection. But one could "demonstrate," with less suppression of counterevidence than many accounts of his books have employed, that one or the other of these two views is superior to all other possibilities. Does he not, first, reveal in every line that he is *best* viewed as an instrument for changing the lives of his readers? Muted as his polemic may be by his ironic style, his life's work cannot be understood as other than a noble effort to change our ways of thinking about science, poetry, and history, our views of their history and of the universe in which we pursue them. Abrams has often said that he is *not* attempting to proselytize for any one view of the world. But consider such a statement as this about the "necessary condition for any full understanding of the past."

In *Natural Supernaturalism* I tried, by an effort of imagination, to understand a great Romantic enterprise by looking at it from within. In the process of coming to understand this segment of our past I also discovered, and tried at the end to communicate the discovery, that to know who and what and where we were then helps us to understand who and what and where we are now. I tried in addition to communicate my sense that this Romantic past is a *usable* past, in that it presents a stance toward ourselves and the

world which affirms human dignity and the grounds for a qualified hope, and thus shows us *what was possible* for men who were
no less sagacious and unillusioned than we are now [my italics].[9]

If this is not using history as an instrument, a tool for changing
minds and spirits, I can't think what would be.
But with equal ease one could show his claims as the poet or
sculptor, the maker of beautiful shapes. *Natural Supernaturalism,*
he tells us, is "iconic of the spiral form which many Romantic
thinkers considered the necessary shape of all intellection."[10]
When I asked him a while ago to comment in print on his historical method, he wrote: "The reason for my silence [on my own
methods] is simple: these books were not written with any
method in mind. Instead they were conceived, researched,
worked out, put together, pulled apart, and put back together,
not according to a theory of valid procedures in such under-
takings, but by intuition. I relied, that is, on my sense of rightness and wrongness, of doubt and assurance, of deficiencies and
superfluities, of what is appropriate and what is inappropriate."[11] What is this but an invitation to view the historian,
after all, as a *maker,* a maker of shapes to be appreciated as
shape, as form? If I took seriously this metaphor of poet, of
maker, would I not find a different Abrams than the one revealed when I pursue the mirror or the instrument?

The Lamp

When we look at that last quotation in context, however, we
discover a more plausible rival to the mirror-historian. He continues like this:

> I should like to think that these intuitions were the kind that Col-
> eridge describes, which follow from "such a knowledge of the facts,
> material and spiritual, that most appertain to [the writer's] art, as,

[9]*CI,* pp. 463-64; *CU,* p. 194.
[10]*CI,* p. 450; *CU,* p. 179.
[11]*CI,* p. 447; *CU,* p. 176.

if it have been governed and applied by *good sense*, and rendered instinctive by habit, becomes the representative and reward of our past conscious reasonings, insights, and conclusions, and acquires the name of TASTE." We must distinguish between ignorant intuitions and those which are the reward of prior experience, reading, and thinking; the play of this latter class of intuitions is what we mean by expertise.

In retrospect, I think I was right to compose ... by relying on taste, tact, and intuition rather than on a controlling method. A book ... , which deals with the history of human intellection, feeling, and imagination, employs special vocabularies, procedures, and modes of demonstration which, over many centuries of development, have shown their profitability when applied to matters of this sort.[12]

Though this statement does not repudiate accurate mirroring, its emphasis is on intuition of "spiritual" matters, and it thus seems to me to claim the powers we might call *lamping*. As lamp-historian, he says, he worked by *intuition*, relied on his *sense* of rightness and wrongness, on his *taste*, on his *expertise*. Since these four qualities belong to him, many of us readers cannot fully share them; in relying on them, he claims to cast a light from an inner source inaccessible to our appraisal, and thus to reveal more than any simple mirror could.

Is not Abrams, as manifold creator of icons of Romanticism, himself to be viewed as he reports Lussky reporting Schlegel reporting Shakespeare: "just as God, despite His transcendence, is immanent in the world, showing 'the invisible things of him ... by the things that are made,' so also the typical modern writer, Shakespeare ... , despite his transcendence of his works by virtue of his objectivity [read: accurate mirroring], is plainly immanent in them and reveals his invisible presence by the things that he has made."[13] So his history could best be viewed as a unique illumination flowing from this man, and thus revealing his own special richness in his special time.

[12]*CI*, pp. 447-48; *CU*, p. 176.
[13]*The Mirror and the Lamp* (New York, 1953), p. 240.

The Master Ophthalmologist

We might, then, rest content with thinking of him as an especially complex union of lamps and mirrors—his intuition doing its lamping merely by casting a nondistorting natural light—were it not for his frequent statements about pluralism. At the beginning of *The Mirror and the Lamp* he says, "There are . . . many profitable ways to approach the history of criticism." But he does not say what the approaches will be, other than his own "analysis of basic metaphors." Criticism is inherently plural, as Chapter 1 of that book insists, and its plurality can be properly explored by "bringing of submerged analogies into the open" and thus putting "certain old facts into a new and . . . revealing perspective."[14] But what, then, of literary history?

Recently he has carried the metaphor of perspective further:

> All sound attempts to add to our humanistic understanding are written from some one of various possible perspectives or points of view (the recourse to optical metaphors is almost inevitable in discussing such matters), and the convergence of diverse perspectives is needed to yield what the philosopher, J. R. Bambrough, calls a 'vision in depth' in place of the two-dimensional vision that we get from any one vantage point. Only such a vision in depth approximates the full humanistic truth about any matter of our deep concern. That is why . . . it is not just that we should tolerate a plurality of histories, we should demand them.

Accepting the possible truth of accounts of Romanticism that would seem to contradict his own, and even of one that would drop Wordsworth "to the bottom of the scale as the weakest and least representative of the prominent poets in this central mode of the Romantic imagination and achievement," Abrams faces the charge of relativism that such acceptance might raise.

> The disparate judgments about the representative quality and greatness of Wordsworth's poetry . . . follow from different con-

[14]Ibid., p. viii.

trolling categories which effect a different selection and ordering of the historical facts and implicate a different set of criteria by which to assess what is representative and great. The insights and assessments of each book, in other words, are relative to the vantage point chosen by its author, and each tries to make us see selected goings-on in the Romantic era in a certain way; but these diverse goings-on are there to be seen in that way. Each, that is, tells only a *part* of the truth, but it is a part of the *truth*.

But there are an indefinite number of revealing perspectives, and each age will no doubt continue to generate new ones that accord with its interests and intellectual climate. "And that is why . . . the search for humanistic truth has no ending."[15]

And so we have the true confessions of a metaphorist after all, though a reluctant one: "the recourse to optical metaphors is almost inevitable in discussing such matters." But the recourse to optical metaphors, let alone the metaphor of multiple perspectives, was *not* inevitable to critics discussing poetry in the extended history he traces: they had found pragmatic and expressive and objective metaphors also applicable, often even preferable; nor was perspectivism inevitable to Abrams as he traced those critics. It seems inevitable to him only now as he discusses the plurality of historical methods and accounts.

Why does optical perspectivism seem the only plausible metaphor for Abrams describing Abrams? Are there no serious rivals?

First we should note that the metaphor does not in itself determine which end of the multiple telescopes or microscopes we look through, or how much distortion we attribute to various lens grinders or eye doctors. You could say that Abrams usually sees his subject (except, that is, when he is driven to talk about pluralism) as the landscape itself, which is "there to be seen," and not the interesting peculiar powers and limitations of the lens that unfortunately picks up only one perspective. On the other

[15]*CI,* pp. 459–60; *CU,* pp. 189–90.

hand, *I* am making that lens my subject here and for the moment accepting the perspective metaphor, as do all of the currently fashionable "reader-critics" and advocates of indeterminacy of meaning.[16] In doing so we are obviously no longer talking of mirrors; though his subject is the landscape, it is an indeterminately distorted one, and *my* subject, Abrams, begins to sound again like an especially complicated version of those poets-as-lamps: he streams forth part of himself upon the landscape, and thus makes the color filters and polarizations of light that belong to him at least as interesting a part of reality as what they reveal. But he professes to allow an indeterminate number of quite different perspective machines. It is thus scarcely surprising that he has been often charged with relativism. If the number of acceptable perspectives is itself not determinable from some superior perspective, why are not the meaning-multipliers right after all? Is there no standard of taste in perspectives?

We have seen enough by now to say that if there is a standard, it will be itself metaphorical. Despite Abrams' claims to literal mirroring, we have lost all hope of appraising his views, as compared with other possible views, without the use of metaphor. Abrams clearly believes that some perspectives are superior to others, and that the very metaphor of perspectivism itself is superior to views that imply a single fixed history: "the search for humanistic truth has no ending."

The Actor in Process

If we think about what it is that has no ending in that formulation, we come to what may seem the most plausible placement of Abrams as historian: he is a step, a stage, a stride, a moment.

---

[16]For a cogent history of perspective as a metaphor—from visual to intellectual—see Claudio Guillén, "On the Concept and Metaphor of Perspective," in *Comparatists at Work: Studies in Comparative Literature,* ed. Stephen G. Nichols, Jr., and Richard B. Vowles (Waltham, Mass., 1968), pp. 29–90. For an intensive critique of the metaphor as it tempts toward relativism, see E. D. Hirsch, *The Aims of Interpretation* (Chicago, 1976), chap. 3.

What he mirrors is process, and the mirror itself moves. His lamp is potentially many lamps, and their natures shift as time passes. His books, as we have seen, flow into being without rigorous blueprint, and they enter a flux that he will not allow anyone to freeze. Surely we should think of him as in motion recording others in motion.

It should not surprise us that as a maker of charts and applier of labels Abrams simply left this whole domain out. He gives us no place for the literary critic who does what I have elsewhere argued Abrams himself does, the critic who celebrates the poem as essentially a culminating (or focal) moment in a historical process, and who demonstrates the poet's greatness by showing him as essentially a moving center of forces flowing from the past into the future. He thus provides no place for himself as historian.

I shall not repeat here my argument that Abrams' history of Wordsworth's poem is an original and powerful critical act demonstrating the poem's greatness by discovering the history it embodies.[17] I must simply build from that claim, as an assumption here, and continue to seek appropriate metaphors for that strange kind of literary-criticism-as-history. In contrast to the mirrors, lamps, instruments, and sculptors that Abrams traced, we find ourselves thinking of him here as a step or stride, a climax, even a crisis; or a rung on a ladder, or staircase perhaps, especially a spiral staircase. Just as a poem, in the historicist view, can be a giant or petty stride forward or backward, a step up or down the ladder of history (leading to accounts of the rise or fall of whole cultures), and just as a critical view can both deal with the poem as moment and *be* a moment in the time stream of criticism, so the historian's work can both describe poems and critical acts as strides or moments and itself be thought of as a step in history.

To view him in this way would be simply to take seriously his

[17]*CI*, pp. 431–34; *CU*, pp. 159–62.

way of viewing the figures he treats. And it would be to read him as following from and leading to a multiplicity of historians and cultural forces unique to his time. Abrams' histories are themselves events in a history, and they thus bear the unique marks of their moment in time. They simply could not have been conceived at any earlier human moment, as one realizes if one tries to think of their genesis without such antecedents as A. O. Lovejoy's experiments in the history of ideas and various twentieth-century formulations of critical pluralism. If Abrams is in any sense not just a historian but a historicist, his historicism is unlike any earlier historicism, and if he is a pluralist, his pluralism is combined with his historicism in a way that makes it differ strongly from all synchronic pluralisms of the kind developed by his friend Ronald Crane, who viewed rival criticisms as relatively discrete modes, permanent resources available to anyone in any period. Abrams by comparison historicizes every question he treats. Yet he does so while claiming to repudiate relativism, whether concerning historical truth or literary values. What kind of historicism is that?

The Judge

Abrams often describes himself as radically neutral, and if we took him at his word we might indeed rest content with a view of him as essentially an inessentialist, a historicist who is himself committed to nothing permanent as he moves into and out of lives that were themselves in flux. Indeed he has resisted decisively my suggestion that in *Natural Supernaturalism* he relies in part on an unacknowledged faith in permanent values: he is, he says, a "nominalist" who uses all abstract terms, including value terms, as "an expository convenience."[18] "I didn't intend . . . to posit eternal ideas or universal traits of human nature to explain the relations between the various themes and structures that I identify and trace through time. I took care, in fact, to assert

[18]*CI*, p. 450; *CU*, p. 179.

early on that the history I undertook to tell [in *Natural Super-naturalism*] is strictly culture-bound."[19]

The final clause is not deliberately ambiguous: Abrams clearly means that those whose story he recounts were culture-bound, and he does not intend a reference to his own historical act. To be consistent he must think of himself as equally culture-bound as he writes his account, yet there is no hint that when he calls himself a nominalist he thinks of *that* assertion as in any sense unstable, subject to being swept away the next moment in the floodwaters of history. He is as decisive about not being a relativist as he is about being a nominalist and about treating his various figures with neutrality.

Something must give here, and something does give: the claim to neutrality will not hold, it will not hold at all. For one thing, the claim to nominalism is itself a violation of neutrality, since many of the figures he traces, perhaps most, were in some sense essentialists or "realists." Even if we take that objection as a quibble, it is still inescapable that Abrams is not neutral in his account. First, he judges some of the statements he reports as superior to others. Try as he will, he cannot conceal from us his conviction that some Romantic ideas are less capricious or harmful, have more lasting value, achieve a closer "match" to human nature and our possibilities than others. When he talks of his selected Romantics' *usability*, praises them for affirming "human dignity and the grounds for a qualified hope," and judges them as "no less sagacious" than we are, either the talk of grounds, hope, and sagacity means something real or it does not. When he calls the Romantics powerful, convincing, fair, and deliberately affirmative in their choice of hope over despair, his own choice is clear—and it is clearly not in his view a *mere* leap of blind faith. And to believe in the validity of such statements is not, as I see it, compatible with a pure nominalism.

Second, his own account, as one perspective, is asserted to

[19]*CI*, p. 453; *CU*, p. 182.

have truth value, the value, at the very least, of mirroring something that not only was truly *there* but is somehow *there* still—wherever "there" is. Even when we decide that all literary history is radically metaphorical, either the metaphors have truth value or they do not.

It would no doubt be a mistake to worry very much about what terms we use here, but the nominalist–realist conflict cannot simply be shoved under the pluralist rug. When Abrams claims to be a nominalist who simply uses concepts as a convenience, I think he understates the challenge his own history presents to those who would reject it by writing other versions of the same events. My suggestion of "platonic" ideas worried him, so I shall here moderate my charge of "realism" and claim only that he is a realist at least in the sense meant by Karl Popper when he argues for the real existence of what he calls "world three." World one is the world of objects, tables and chairs. World two is our experience of these objects, including our ways of forming concepts from our perceptions. World three is the world of our statements about them—most obviously the world of printed statement.but also our speech to each other. Popper's argument is not of course simply that books, as physical objects, and speech, as sound waves, exist, but that propositions, problems, arguments, and theories are real, as real as tables and chairs.[20] For many reasons, only some of which Popper covers, I think it is inescapable both that world three is real, often as solid as rocks in its effects on our lives, and that Abrams believes it to be real. Popper, unlike Abrams, argues that the real ideas of world three, the problems we try to solve, the theories we propound, the arguments we offer, are, if unambiguously true, true forever and thus timeless; but Popper resists the next step, taken by Plato, which says that we do not, as human beings, invent these things but discover them. While Abrams is decisive about not

---

[20]Popper's arguments for the reality of world three can be found everywhere in his later work. See especially chap. 38, "World 3 or the Third World," in *Unended Quest: An Intellectual Autobiography* (London: Fontana, 1976).

consorting with such permanent forms, he clearly believes that the ideas he traces are real in precisely Popper's sense of realism: they act on the world as ideas; they have consequences; they have a life of their own.

Those biblical notions of eternal salvation came spiraling through the lives of the Romantics and caused them, in direct encounters with other powerful ideas, to develop a new secular version of salvation. That version in turn went on spiraling down through the nineteenth century and into Abrams' books, as you might say, where they are so real that they have produced his critics' responses, his responses in turn, and finally this very real moment here and now. For Plato, though not for Popper, only the small part of all of this that will prove permanent is really real. But it is important to see that at least in Popper's terms ideas as Abrams traces them *are* reality, and that since both those ideas and the tracing of them are *metaphoric,* metaphors are not simply distorting pictures of reality: they are pieces of reality. Or at least they can be.

When we put even this limited realism together with Abrams' obvious willingness to assert that some statements are superior to other statements, he emerges, it seems to me, as a curious and wonderful kind of judge—that is, a critic, a critic of historical metaphor. He clearly believes—though I am not at all sure that I could get him to stand up in meeting and say so—that one can show, by his special kind of narrative, the superiority of some metaphoric views or perspectives over others. As a master of his kind of cultural history, he is thus best viewed, we can now argue, as a master critic of man's grandest metaphoric visions. To read and respond to his work is to reject, radically and un-ambiguously, any intellectual history that would reduce the world to what Popper calls worlds one and two: objects and concepts of objects. All mechanistic histories, all histories based on economic determinism, all histories that see ideas as epiphenomena and metaphors as at best pretty decorations on the real cake, something "literally real"—all are shown by his work to be absurd impoverishments of reality.

What is more, Abrams' chosen view of how Romantics secularized the myth of Christian salvation can be viewed as an
incisive criticism of all other possible views of how our culture
changed its mind. His account of deconversion from the Christian view and of what we can call reconversion to natural supernaturalism criticizes all other possibilities. Though he is quite
justified in saying that other valid accounts of Romanticism
could be constructed, I think he modestly understates the sense
in which his book will stand in judgment upon them: just as he
will not accept any and all readings of any one of his authors, his
books repudiate many—though not all—alternative histories of
the period. In effect they prophesy, by their cogency, that only a
limited number will survive their day in a court that he has
constituted. But with the notion of *constituting*, we are no longer
dealing merely with the judge.

The Maker of Constitutions

It is the nature of metaphoric truth that our criteria for judg-
ing it should be imprecise, and that more than one metaphoric
account of the same phenomenon—in this case M. H.
Abrams—will survive the criticism offered by all the other accounts. I said earlier that one little collection of metaphors for
Abrams—as Waring blender and bottle opener and so on—
seemed obviously deficient, even though each metaphor conveyed some truth about our man. My exploration of other possible metaphors will have suggested—it cannot have proved—
both that some metaphors for his kind of work are better than
others and that we cannot and should not be satisfied with only
one: we are not able finally to pin him wriggling to some one
part of the chart of "positions" that I derived from his own
schema.

A good way to summarize what we have learned of him under
our various metaphors might be to reconsider one that I merely
touched on earlier: the historian as "sculptor" or "maker." The
metaphor seemed to offer little illumination because we took the
things made, or shaped, as only the texts he has written. Suppose

we ask instead what it is that Abrams really made as he "conceived, researched, worked out, put together, pulled apart, and put back together" what was ostensibly a book.

Implicit in what I have said are, it seems to me, at least the following "acts of constitution," makings of realities that were only *potentially* "there" before:

• A new M. H. Abrams. The person we are honoring was in large part shaped by the task of writing the books. He did not know or believe when he began what he knew and believed when he finished. The writing thus remade the man, the so-called real Abrams (whom his wife presumably knows best), as he discovered what he believed and created the "author" whom most of us come to know.

• A new audience for talk about Romanticism and cultural history in general. As a result of his macrometaphorizing, more of us will think about these matters and care about them than would otherwise have been true.

• A new mode of thought. All of us who read him will think about his various subjects, even if we disagree with many of his conclusions, in ways quite different from our former ways. More of us, for example, will think of the rise of "natural supernaturalism" in the light cast by his metaphoric vision of the spiral, and more of us will think of other subjects metaphorically, in the hope of finding equally compelling pictures of how human events move.

• A new picture of who we are, as heirs to "all that." The reader who enters honestly into Abrams' world—that is, the reader who reads—cannot help emerging with an expanded notion of life and its possibilities, both for the Romantics and for ourselves. Whether the change is great or small, whether it is resisted or embraced, the reconstitution is as inescapable as skin tanning for those who lie in the sun.

One could go on; to do justice to Abrams-as-constitutor-of-reality would require many pages. But the important point is that this final picture of Abrams as maker, as constitutor of new worlds, is not finally in simple rivalry with the others. Though I think it is more nearly adequate than the others, it is clear that he could not make so well if he did not mirror and lamp and manipulate perspective glasses and change in a changing time and—finally—judge. Yet he could do none of these things so well if, like certain other historians of his time, he tempted us to see him as a psephologist, say, or a naughty boy flinging turds, or a juggler, or a magician entertaining us with a levitation act. Thus, though we cannot settle on a single metaphor, the precise list that he has suggested is by no means either capricious or neutral. It is true that every historian we respect, considered as closely as we have considered Abrams, would suggest to us some of the same metaphors. But none would yield the precise *illuminations* of this *critical maker*, M. H. Abrams.

IV

The claim that historical accounts are metaphoric is sure to strike many these days as self-evident and many others as a dangerous threat to the very possibility of historical knowledge.[21] A major value of Abrams' peculiar combination of virtues is that he challenges both of these easy responses. Fashionable views that "everything is metaphor" seem to sanction a careless proliferation of ever newer revisions, with everyman becoming his own historian—and constitution maker—to a degree that would have shocked even Carl Becker.[22] Abrams establishes standards of performance—of rigor and industry and clarity of form—that will always shame those who would substitute creative novelty for depth of specification and care in establishing what Abrams calls "literal" connections. On the other hand,

[21]The deep divisions on this issue are intensely illustrated by Hayden White's *Metahistory: The Historical Imagination in Nineteenth-Century Europe* (Baltimore, 1973) and the responses to it.
[22]I'm thinking of the seemingly almost forgotten work that so shocked me as a young man, *Everyman His Own Historian* (New York, 1935).

those positivists who are fearful that talk of metaphor scuttles cognitive claims may discover a new view of human possibility if they will simply turn to his texts and read them carefully. If my reduction of his grand reductions of the irreducible richness of our past is worrisome to them, Abrams himself should convince anyone who follows him line by line that at least one tough cognitive test has been met: though it is through metaphor that we learn what he teaches, we know that if Abrams is right, many others must be wrong.

If the ability to make metaphors is, as Aristotle claims, the greatest poetic gift of all, the ability to create macrometaphor is surely the greatest of intellectual gifts. Each of the major philosophies may be viewed, as Stephen C. Pepper argued almost forty years ago, as rooted in a grand metaphor that has survived criticism by other master metaphorists.[23] In the same spirit we could argue that the great epics and novels and plays are those that have plumbed to our roots and discovered the patterns that can *stand for* or serve as critical versions of human life and its possibilities. What I am arguing here is that great cultural histories such as Abrams' are similarly masterpieces of grand metaphor: they do not so much tell us what happened in our past as reveal to us what our past *was like:* it was *like* this immeasurably rich, subtle, emotion-rich, and poetry-ridden picture that Abrams offers—and it was, by the same token, *not* really much like those pictures other historians have offered.

Such revelations of course create for us as readers crises of judgment, not just about the past but about life itself. When Abrams shows us in his spiral history of spiraling events that his Romantics had engaged in a "bold and deliberate enterprise," and that their embrace of the Romantic "positives," "Of Truth, of Grandeur, Beauty, Love, and Hope, / And melancholy Fear subdued by Faith" was at least as reasonable as the fashionable

[23]Stephen C. Pepper, *World Hypotheses: A Study in Evidence* (Berkeley, 1942).

nihilisms of our time, he is in effect rehabilitating one plausible way of living in a troubled world.

Can life be affirmed without lapsing into unreason? Abrams the metaphorist shows us that it can be, since his protagonists have in fact done it. He also modestly shows himself as performing in our time two grand positive acts—the writing of his histories—achievements that in themselves challenge the notion that we must choose between those two oversimplified metaphoric visions of the human condition: our ancestors' notion that unless we can hope for a heavenly city we are doomed to eternal hellfire, and our contemporaries' notion that unless we can hope for a perfecting of the secular order we must live in despair.

A Coleridgean Criticism of the Work of M. H. Abrams

THOMAS MCFARLAND

I intend to speak in this essay not merely about the contribution of M. H. Abrams to the study of English literature, but also about the larger question of the relation of his work to the structure of literary canonicity. The adjective "Coleridgean" in the title of the paper is invoked to indicate that the discussion will be concerned more with the elucidation of principles than with the examination of particularities. For if it is true that Coleridge is the greatest of English critics, it is also true that he is not very much like the other competitors for that accolade. His Shakespearean criticism, for instance, is of little pedagogic use, because it does not comprehensively analyze the plays. Rather it selects certain texts to illustrate systematic principles of literary conception. The quiddity of a work under discussion is almost invariably subordinate in Coleridge's critical procedure to the conclusions he seeks to exemplify—as is apparent from, say, the fifteenth chapter of the *Biographia Literaria,* which is about the specific symptoms of poetic power to be found in Shakespeare's *Venus and Adonis.*

Such an idea of criticism stands in radical antithesis to the antiphilosophical close reading of F. R. Leavis, or the coherence criticism of Cleanth Brooks. As T. S. Eliot noted with some puzzlement in *The Sacred Wood,* though "Coleridge was perhaps the greatest of English critics, and in a sense the last," and though his "natural abilities," and some of his performances, are "probably more remarkable than those of any other modern critic," he is nevertheless characteristically "apt to take leave of the data of criticism, and arouse the suspicion that he has been diverted into a metaphysical hare-and-hounds. His end does not always appear to be the return to the work of art with improved perception and intensified, because more conscious, enjoyment.... In the derogatory sense he is more 'philosophic' than Aristotle. For everything that Aristotle says illuminates the literature which is the occasion for saying it; but Coleridge only now and then."

To Coleridge, moreover, the simple fact that the term "criticism" can be proposed for a work is in itself a sign of the high importance of that work, because he believed that only a few productions deserve to be criticized. The larger portion by far simply need to be catalogued, tabulated, and described. Accordingly, though it would be paradoxical, it would not be entirely inappropriate to say that the task of criticizing the work of M. H. Abrams from a Coleridgean standpoint is adequately served simply when the topic of criticism is put forward; for by using the word "criticism" in a Coleridgean sense I am saying first of all that the *oeuvre* of Abrams is among the most serious, weighty, and important achievements of American humanistic learning.

Still, even without invoking the Coleridgean adjective, to use the word "criticism" as I intend it here is not to use it in the sense in which it would apply, say, to commentary on Shakespeare. In truth, in the sense in which I intend the term, it would be fair to say that there is virtually no Shakespearean criticism being produced today, and even that there has been none for many decades now. The proper term for our contemporary approaches to Shakespeare is, to adopt the distinction propounded by G. Wilson Knight in *The Wheel of Fire,* "interpretation," not "criticism." As Knight said:

THOMAS MCFARLAND

'Criticism' to me suggests a certain process of deliberately objectify-
ing the work under consideration; the comparison of it with other
similar works in order especially to show in what respect it sur-
passes, or falls short of, those works; the dividing its 'good' from its
'bad'; and, finally, a formal judgment as to its lasting validity. 'Interpretation,' on the contrary, tends to merge into the work it
analyses; it attempts, as far as possible, to understand its subject in
the light of its own nature, employing external reference, if at all,
only as a preliminary to understanding; it avoids discussion of
merits, and, since its existence depends entirely on its original
acceptance of the validity of the poetic unit which it claims, in some
measure, to translate into discursive reasoning, it can recognize no
division of 'good' from 'bad.' Thus criticism is active and looks
ahead, often treating past work as material on which to base future
standards and canons of art; interpretation is passive, and looks
back, regarding only the imperative challenge of a poetic vision.
Criticism is a judgment of vision; interpretation a reconstruction of
vision.

Not only is almost all so-called Shakespearean criticism actually
interpretation, but in those rare instances where criticism is in
fact attempted, the results are likely to be disastrous. I have in
mind a recent book by a scholar named French, which starts
from the unexceptionable premise that even Shakespeare sometimes nodded, and then proceeds to ascribe fault to various
Shakespearean tropes when actually, at least to my mind, the
critic simply fails to understand them satisfactorily.

If the criticism of such giants as Shakespeare, Dante, and
Homer tends in the event to be interpretation, almost all of the
criticism that occurs in journals tends to be either mediation or
tabulation. In any case, it is not what Coleridge meant by criticism. Book reviews, whether in such sophisticated general journals as *TLS* and *The New York Review of Books* or in such special
scholarly repositories as *JEGP*, exist mainly as a means of keep-
ing track of the influx of new culture. In doing so, they render
the counterservice to new books of—well, in a word—advertising
them. Nor is this function, in either of its aspects, a negligible
one. As Hazlitt said in his essay "On Criticism":

A Coleridgean Criticism of the Work of M. H. Abrams

> The truth is, that in the quantity of works that issue from the press, it is utterly impossible they should all be read by all sorts of people. There must be *tasters* for the public, who must have a discretionary power vested in them, for which it is difficult to make them properly accountable. Authors in proportion to their numbers become not formidable, but despicable. They would not be heard of or severed from the crowd without the critic's aid, and all complaints of ill-treatment are vain.

With the exponential increase in intellectual publication, the tasting use of criticism becomes more and more indispensable to any cohesive intellectual life.

The watershed between interpretation and tasting is constituted by canonicity, which is a conception both very little addressed by contemporary thought, and one that is rapidly increasing in importance. If a work is in the canon, it is a fit subject for interpretation; if it is not in the canon, it is presented to the intellectual public by some version or other of tasting. The tasting function simulates criticism, but it is hardly criticism in the Coleridgean sense. It usually proceeds more or less along the lines laid down by Hazlitt: "At first, it is generally satisfied to give an opinion whether a work is good or bad, and to quote a passage or two in support of this opinion: afterwards, it is bound to assign the reasons of its decision and to analyze supposed beauties or defects with microscopic minuteness." Though such treatment assumes the form of criticism, it is not criticism, for reasons that I hope will become plainer in the next few paragraphs of argument.

When we think of canonicity, and the special privilege that canonicity confers on an author's work, the question arises, and doubtless for most of us with considerable urgency, how does work pass from the status of transient offering to the status of canonical permanence? Or, to put the matter another way, what intermediate process takes place between the cultural consideration described as tasting and the cultural consideration described as interpretation?

The answer to both questions is contained in the word "criticism"; and criticism may by the same token be comprehensively defined as the process by which canonicity is conferred on cultural offerings. Alternatively, we may say that every canonical figure's status as subject of interpretation must necessarily be preceded by criticism.

There are variations and complexities here that make one wary of too easy a schematism. For instance, the New Criticism was not, at least as I understand it, properly speaking a criticism, but rather a mode of pedagogic interpretation; and its most striking success was in classroom elucidations. It worked almost exclusively in terms of the received canon and was in fact largely an attempt to wrest the canon away from the scholarly practitioners of a predominantly historical tabulation.

In truth, the New Criticism necessarily had to work in terms of the received canon, because it lacked an essential component of criticism as such: that is, learning. The Coleridges, Arnolds, Aristotles, and Schlegels of the world have all been extraordinarily learned men. (I have always been intrigued by Wilhelm Schlegel, who, after heroic contributions to the magnificent German translation of Shakespeare and equally profound and linguistically adept comprehensions of the literatures of Greece, Rome, Spain, Italy, Portugal, and France—his writings in French alone occupy three volumes, while Stendhal judged after reading his lectures that he didn't "believe anyone can know ancient Greece and its poets better"—after all this mastered Sanskrit and translated both the Ramayana and the Bhagavad-Gita into Latin.) Indeed, learning and critical competence have traditionally been linked together. As Addison observed in 1712, in *Spectator* 291: "The Truth of it is, there is nothing more absurd, than for a Man to set up for a Critick, without a good Insight into all the Parts of Learning"; and he says that were he to choose his readers

by whose Judgment I would stand or fall, they should not be such as are acquainted only with the *French* and *Italian* Criticks, but also with the Antient and Moderns who have written in either of the learned Languages. Above all, I would have them well versed in the *Greek* and *Latin* Poets. . . . Nor is it sufficient, that a Man who sets up for a Judge in Criticism, should have perused the Authors above-mentioned, unless he has also a clear and logical Head. Without this Talent he is perpetually puzzled and perplexed amidst his own Blunders, mistakes the Sense of those he would confute, or if he chances to think right, does not know how to convey his Thoughts to another with Clearness and Perspicuity. *Aristotle,* who was the best Critick, was also one of the best Logicians that ever appeared in the World.

But in America in the 1930s, with a preliminary school system devastated by the application of John Dewey's educational theories, few students possessed such qualifications. By the tenets of the New Criticism, however, an aspiring candidate, despite his lack of a "good Insight into all the Parts of Learning," could, by the tactful manipulation of a few relatively self-contained conceptions such as irony and ambiguity, set himself up reasonably as a functioning critic—heartened at the outset by R. P. Blackmur's definition of "criticism" as "the formal discourse of an amateur."

I myself should think, on the contrary, entirely in accord with Addison, that the true critic is the most professional of all those who contribute to the world of literature; and that learning is the preparatory condition of that professionalism. Even Edmund Wilson, who seems more a cultivated taster than either a critic or an interpreter, or Sainte-Beuve, who oscillated between tasting and interpretation, possessed learning—Sainte-Beuve, of course, a goodly portion of it. In this respect, the massive and detailed learning of such a cultural figure as M. H. Abrams better qualifies him for the title of critic than does the merely declared aspiration of a host of other figures. And yet I do not think of Abrams as being exactly or at any rate predominantly a critic, nor do I think his work is such as ordinarily qualifies for the exercise of criticism upon it. If my audience will bear with me through a fairly lengthy circuit of argument, I shall attempt to resolve these paradoxes, or at least illuminate them.

What defines the critic absolutely, as opposed to the taster or interpreter, is an involvement with the conferring of canonicity. In this understanding perhaps one could advance, against Blackmur's espousal of amateurism, a formal definition of criticism as "the learned judgment of a work on the threshold of the canon." Francis Jeffrey, for instance, seems to me neither a taster nor an interpreter, but unequivocally a critic, even if a bad one. As Leslie Stephen remarks in his essay "The First Edinburgh Reviewers":

> In the last of his poetical critiques (October 1829) [Jeffrey] sums up his critical experience.... "The tuneful quartos of Southey," he says, "are already little better than lumber; and the rich melodies of Keats and Shelley, and the fantastical emphasis of Wordsworth, and the plebeian pathos of Crabbe, are melting fast from the field of vision. The novels of Scott have put out his poetry. Even the splendid strains of Moore are fading into distance and dimness... and the blazing star of Byron himself is receding from its place of pride." Who survives this general decay? Not Coleridge, who is not even mentioned.... The two who show least marks of decay are—of all people in the world—Rogers and Campbell! It is only to be added that this summary was republished in 1843, by which time the true proportions of the great reputations of the period were becoming more obvious to an ordinary observer. It seems almost incredible now that any sane critic should pick out the poems of Rogers and Campbell as the sole enduring relics from the age of Wordsworth, Shelley, Keats, Coleridge, and Byron.

Jeffrey thus seems like an usher who haughtily misreads the credentials of those seeking entry to the canon; but an usher is not less an usher when he is turning away a would-be entrant than when he is escorting that figure to an honored seat. It is always the case, however, that the usher is not in himself the authorizing judge of admissibility. He is rather the final link in a chain of validation.

Every critic, in short, no matter how much of the tone of peremptory *ipse dixit* may seem to invest his individual judgments, derives his authority from the strength of a collective process. Jeffrey's judgments failed in their canonical function not because they were wrong—if by wrong one is speaking of some kind of scientifically ascertainable objectivity—but because they were solipsistically at variance with the collective process. Leavis, following Eliot, defines criticism, in *The Common Pursuit,* as " 'the common pursuit of true judgment': that is how the critic should see his business, and what it should be for him. His perceptions and judgments are his, or they are nothing; but, whether or not he has consciously addressed himself to cooperative labour, they are inevitably collaborative. Collaboration may take the form of disagreement, and one is grateful to the critic whom one has found worth disagreeing with." I may add parenthetically that not the least of the services of Harold Bloom for my own understanding of literature has been his demonstration of how various are the ways in which cultural endeavor we customarily think of as individual is in fact collective.

We can, I think, discern in the collaborative effort of criticism a more definite structure than Leavis ascribes to it. Two distinct moments seem to occur in the group process by which a work or a body of work is ushered into the canon. The first is the concurring judgments of more than one established critic. Thus three great critical efforts established Wordsworth firmly in the canon: the first was Coleridge's criticism in the *Biographia Literaria;* the second was Arnold's introduction to a selection of Wordsworth's poetry, known more familiarly as the chapter in *Essays in Criticism; Second Series;* and the third was Bradley's essay in the *Oxford Lectures on Poetry.* Bradley's piece was written in the first decade of our own century, by which time the process of criticism was already shading over into interpretation. And since that time only interpretation has had an audience. The great revival of Wordsworth studies in the present era, signalized by but not restricted to the books of John Jones and David Ferry and Geoffrey Hartman, consists almost entirely of interpretation.

THOMAS McFARLAND

Of course there were other Wordsworthian criticisms, and distinguished ones, in addition to those of Coleridge, Arnold, and Bradley. The perceptive comments of Hazlitt, for instance, represent criticism of a high order. I specify Coleridge, Arnold, and Bradley, however, in order to illustrate the truth that the critical concurrence must be spread out over a vertical progression in time; and in this respect Hazlitt's criticism, keen though it is, is supererogatory.

The second moment in the collective process by which a figure or body of work is ushered into the canon consists of what Coleridge called variously "a mental antecedent," a "pre-cogitation," and a "previous act and conception of the mind." He used these terms when talking in *The Friend* about the structure of method, but we may extrapolate them for the critical process and say that there must be conditioning judgments beforehand by which the actual work of criticism is in effect telling the intellectual public something to which it has already assented. The situation, to marshal a political analogy, is something like a legislator bringing to a formal vote on the floor a topic already settled in cloakroom consultations beforehand. Thus Shakespeare was established for the nineteenth century in England largely by the criticism of Coleridge; but before Coleridge, as R. W. Babcock has urged in *The Genesis of Shakespeare Idolatry*, there were Romantically formative and similar judgments by Maruice Morgann that effectively served as "pre-cogitation" and "mental antecedent." This interweaving process of "pre-cogitation" and authoritative criticism, indeed, constitutes the historical warp and woof of Shakespeare's canonicity. For instance, we may take Ben Jonson's praise in the First Folio as the primary enabling act of Shakespearean criticism. It is stated in a context of extensive learning on Jonson's part—which, as I have argued, is always necessary to critical authority—and it directly concerns itself with the comparative placement that constitutes the canon:

I will not lodge thee by
Chaucer, or Spenser, or bid Beaumont lye

A Coleridgean Criticism of the Work of M. H. Abrams

> A little further, to make thee a roome:
> Thou art a Moniment, without a tombe.

Shakespeare is ranked above Marlowe, Lyly, and Kyd; and with Aeschylus, Euripides, and Sophocles. Jonson asserts

> ... how far thou didst our Lily out-shine,
> Or sporting Kid, or Marlowes mighty line

and says that he might

> ... call forth thund'ring Aeschilus,
> Euripides, and Sophocles

And after such comparison, he concludes with the absolute judgment that Shakespeare "was not of an age, but for all time."

But such exercise of canonical placement, early though it was, was preceded by mental antecedents and pre-cogitation on the part of others. Thus Meres, in 1598, said that "Shakespeare among the English is the most excellent" for both tragedy and comedy; Gabriel Harvey in about 1601 noted privately that "the younger sort takes much delight in Shakespeare's Venus & Adonis: but his Lucrece, & his tragedie of Hamlet, Prince of Denmarke, have it in them, to please the wiser sort." Still more revealing is the formative pre-cogitation presented in the Parnassus Trilogy around 1600, where Gull says, "Let this duncified worlde esteem of Spencer and Chaucer, I'le worshipp sweet Mr. Shakespeare"; and Will Kempe pointedly appends: "Few of the university men pen plaies well, they smell too much of that writer Ovid, and that writer Metamorphosis ... Why here our fellow Shakespeare puts them all down, I and Ben Jonson too."

The second enabling act of criticism was Dryden's, but the pre-cogitative concurrence had grown in the interim, with such things as Mr. Hales of Eton arguing to Ben Jonson, in 1637: "Mr. Hales, who had sat still for some time, hearing Ben frequently reproaching [Shakespeare] with the want of Learning . . . told him at last . . . that if he would produce any one Topick finely treated by any of [the ancients], he would undertake to shew something upon the same Subject at least as well written by Shakespeare." Three years later Leonard Digges stated even more emphatically that Shakespeare was "the patterne of all wit, / Art without Art unparaleld as yet." When Dryden produced his great criticism of 1668, therefore, he was in a sense simply harvesting such opinions; indeed, after saying that Shakespeare "was the man who of all modern, and perhaps ancient poets, had the largest and most comprehensive soul," he starts talking about Shakespeare's topics and actually refers to Mr. Hales of Eton by name.

I have cited this Shakespeareana at some length in order to illustrate and delimit as clearly as possible the nature and extent of any critic's authority. A critic who oversteps these socially cumulative boundaries, under the illusion that his authority resides in his own arbitrary and untrammeled judgment, immediately loses his effect. Thus Yvor Winters becomes as it were the critical equivalent of a drivel and a show when he presents the solipsistic judgment, in his *Forms of Discovery,* that Greville is a better poet than Donne, or that Keats's Nightingale Ode is a "mediocre poem," or that Wordsworth "is a very bad poet who nevertheless wrote a few good lines." In truth, though Winters is doubtless a more important critic than Jeffrey, judgments such as these from critical isolation make him sound no less obtuse than Jeffrey.

By now additional aspects of what I mean by a Coleridgean criticism of the work of M. H. Abrams should have begun to emerge to view. By proposing him as an object for criticism I am proposing him for entry into the canon. At the same time, because of the collective nature of the critical enterprise, my proposal is necessarily more in the nature of a nomination than a final admission. Furthermore, because Abrams' contribution has been most significantly in the realm of interpretation, it poses special problems in its relation to possible canonicity—problems the unraveling of which will lead us to an augmented understanding of the structure of literary permanence. Now literary activity, taken in its largest range, divides itself into two major categories. On the one hand there is a vast cauldron of literary coming to be and passing away, an ocean of everything from cookbooks and books of etiquette to poems that nobody reads, a waving field of grain whose stalks number in the tens, the hundreds of thousands each decade. The absolute condition of this swarm is ephemerality, and some of its brief remnants are to be viewed in constantly changing supply on the dollar counters of Marboro bookstores (and prices and even the stores themselves also constantly change). The other category, far smaller, is the literature of which note is taken. This in its turn is divided into two parts: the canon, which is small indeed by the standards of busy printing presses the world over, and a considerably larger mass of work that is secondary to the canon, and in fact exists primarily to service the canon. It is necessary to the canon, and the canon is necessary to it. As Shaftesbury said in his *Characteristics:* "I take upon me absolutely to condemn the fashionable and prevailing custom of inveighing against critics as the common enemies, the pests and incendiaries of the commonwealth of Wit and Letters. I assert, on the contrary, that they are the props and pillars of this building; and that without the encouragement and propagation of such a race, we should remain as Gothic architects as ever."

The body of secondary or servicing activity lauded by Shaftesbury is in its turn divided once again, as I have argued, into the threefold distinction of tasting activity, critical activity, and interpretational activity. Each of the three functions serves a separate intellectual need of society. The tasters maintain communication with the vast anonymous grain field of coming to be and passing away, winnowing certain stalks for further consideration, whether that consideration take the form of praise or of dismissal. The two remaining sets of functionaries, the critics and the interpreters, control respectively the entrance into the canon and its uncovering again to the intellectual public. I am beset at times by an Egyptological vision, not unlike the opium dreams of De Quincey, in which these various aspects of literary energy and status all have their parallels. The authors of the vast ephemeral publication seem like the anonymous toilers who lived and died in historical obscurity and worked on the pyramids and in the fields. The tasters are like the Egyptian aristocracy, while the critics and interpreters have each a sacerdotal role, the one being the prophets who annunciate the canon, the other, the priests who mediate it. The figures in the canon itself are the pharaohs, embalmed and treasured up on purpose to a life beyond life.

Once a figure enters the canon, he is no longer open to criticism. Or if thought to be open, he invariably reveals himself as no longer affected by it. Even the most determined critical attempts to dislodge him from the canon become merely further data for his interpretation. Leavis' devastating criticism of Shelley has not vitiated Shelley's canonical status, and the attacks on Milton by Waldock and Empson have simply added to the body of Milton studies. Assuredly not all of the figures in the canon deserve to be there; we no doubt all have our own candidates for eviction—one of mine is Landor and his wretched imaginary conversations—but no critic, not even a pride of critics, is capable of accomplishing such an eviction once canonicity has been conferred.

In only one way can a figure disappear from the canon, and that way has nothing to do with criticism. If we cast our imaginations a thousand—ten thousand—years into the future, we immediately realize that the accumulations of time and the limitations of human attention will in due course squeeze and compress the present canon to make way for new relevances. Only the greatest figures will be remembered, and eventually perhaps not even Shakespeare himself will exist in any memory other than a computer's. But this process, to revert to our Egyptological vision, is as though a pyramid is bulldozed to make way for some high-rise edifice of enormously later situation; no power within the epoch or social framework of Egyptological reality can serve as such a bulldozer.

So no critic and no coalition of critics can evict a figure from the canon. Indeed, criticism of the canon is not only unavailing, but so unfitting that it often recoils upon the critic. We realize that Winters seems eccentric and perhaps even ridiculous precisely because he is trying to apply the process of criticism, which is a threshold process, to figures already across the threshold and inside the canon. The giants, so to speak, have retired within the castle, leaving only windmills for the critic's determined lance. And that lance is determined indeed. "There is almost no intellect in or behind the poems" of Keats, judges Winters. "Matthew Arnold," he judges again, "exhibits the worst faults of the period most of the time: he is sentimental to the point of being lachrymose; he offers the worst pseudo-poetic diction imaginable." "A. C. Swinburne," he judges still again, "wrote no poems that will endure serious reading." All these statements are formulations of critical judgment, but for each figure critical judgment was no longer the relevant cultural process.

The relevant cultural process, once a figure has entered the canon, is to serve as a focal point for the ambitions and the need for recognition of the servicing secondary figures. Each secondary commentator doubles his strength, as it were, by attaching his own claim for recognition to a name already universally known. In due course, any canonical figure accretes a certain body of commentary, which, far from closing him off from further discussion, leads to still further commentary—little communes of scholar-interpreters, moving down through the years attached to the fortunes of a figure in the past.

In such a relation it makes very little difference what the real quality of the focal figure might be; all that counts is how much critical mass, if one may be pardoned the phrase, he has accumulated. A reputation might be stopped either by neglect or by adverse criticism if the latter comes early enough. Once canonicity has been achieved, however, nothing can stop it. The effect is comparable to that of a small snowball rolling down Mont Blanc; by the time it gets halfway down it is a very large snowball, and will incorporate the very objects erected to stop it. A graphic case in point is Norman Fruman's book of a few years ago called *Coleridge, the Damaged Archangel*. The work was a dedicated attack on Coleridge's reputation from almost every possible vantage point, and it received much attention in the press. For a while one would hear from lawyers and stockbrokers at cocktail parties that it was a shame that Coleridge studies had been destroyed by Fruman's attack. What actually happened, however, was entirely predictable to one who understood the dynamics of canonicity; after the initial flurry, Fruman's book was simply incorporated into the body of Coleridge interpretation, where it now generates occasions for still further publication by way of confirmation or rebuttal, and the Coleridge snowball, actually augmented by the addition, rolls downward ever more massively.

Accordingly canonicity, as was suggested earlier in this paper, confers a privileged and actually quite changed status on any body of work that achieves it. But that status is more difficult for some kinds of work to attain than for others. The major bar between Abrams' work and canonical status is neither the quality of the work nor its quantity, but rather, as suggested above, that it already occupies a well-defined cultural position as interpretational commentary. Such a position seems peculiarly inertial; at any rate, it is much more usual for criticism to achieve canonicity than it is for interpretation to do so. We need think only of Arnold's *Essays in Criticism* or Coleridge's *Biographia Literaria* to realize that major criticism, after having served its ushering function for the canon, is quite readily taken up itself into the canon—in somewhat the same way, perhaps, that a distinguished commoner might be rewarded with an hereditary earldom after service to the British crown.

A Coleridgean Criticism of the Work of M. H. Abrams

This kind of transformation, however, is far more rare in the realm of interpretation, for reasons that are doubtless complex and certainly not entirely clear. One is in all likelihood the fact that interpretation is more dependent upon scholarship than is criticism, and scholarship, as a *Wissenschaft*, tends to become obsolete. Most of us, to summon a single illustration, have had occasion to browse through back runs of scholarly journals such as *PMLA* for the twenties and thirties, and many of us have possibly been startled, as was recently the case with me, by the datedness of the majority of the articles.

A second reason for the scarcity of transformations from interpretation to canonicity is one that I have elsewhere formulated in these words: *secondary studies are all equal.* I have been rebuked by at least one audience to which I offered this aphorism, but despite its undoubted hyperbole, I find that I am reluctant to discard it. Perhaps it could be less provocatively rephrased this way: with certain exceptions, it makes little difference, in the formation of cultural learning structures, what secondary materials one appropriates, so long as these materials are appropriated in enough mass to reach what might be called *functional plurality.* The contention pertains both to the necessary incompleteness of any and all learning structures and to the substance of the secondary works themselves. As to the latter, the interchangeability and hence the dispensability of most secondary works are effects of their redundancy. Such redundancy, it seems to me, is the final truth about the vast majority of scholarly interpretations. It is not, as a Leavisian approach would have it, that they are bad, inept, and deserving of contempt—on the contrary, they are almost uniformly the results of much individual labor and painfully acquired expertise—but rather that they simply recombine materials, perspectives, and emphases already in the intellectual public domain.

During one's formative years one is intensely open to secondary aid, but this is true only for those years. As a professional scholar with responsibilities to graduate students, I make some attempt to keep abreast of scholarly publication in two or three areas; but I do so as a professional, not because I feel I need the reading for my own intellectual productivity. Indeed, after a certain point in one's cultural formation, the largest portion of the books one encounters seem to be either restatements, or at least easily anticipated extensions, of what one already knows, or to be mistaken.

The formative process itself, because it is limited in time, must necessarily make do with whatever secondary materials lie at hand. The student of Romanticism in 1935 would read Praz; he would not be able to read Bate. The student of Romanticism in 1950 would read Bate; he would not be able to read Bloom. The inexorable consequence of this temporal limitation in the acquisition of secondary aid is that in, say, the study of Spenser, any half-dozen books on Spenser will do as well as any other six as preparation for significant experience of Spenser himself. To say otherwise is really to say that we cannot approach Spenser at all, for we should always have to defer our reading in expectation of the appearance of future interpretations. In fact, however, not many in the late twentieth century would have the temerity to say they experience Spenser more deeply than did Keats in the early nineteenth; and perhaps none would say he could read him more deeply than did Milton.

So we make use of what the moment provides. Few or none wait for future interpretations, nor should they. The secondary aids available at any time will serve as well as those at any other time.

The contribution of M. H. Abrams to English studies, however, is an exception to this anonymous leveling and interchangeability of scholarly interpretations. Perhaps an anecdote will serve to dramatize this exceptional quality in his work, and at the same time constitute the "previous act and conception" or "pre-cogitation" necessary to criticism itself. When I was an instructor at the University of Virginia in the mid-1950s, the chairman of the department came in one day and presented two of my fellow instructors and myself with a request he had received to list the ten most important nonfiction works in English, pertinent to English studies, of this century. My colleagues and I fell to with a will. By mutual agreement we listed Abrams' *The Mirror and the Lamp* and Lovejoy's *The Great Chain of Being*. When I suggested that Cassirer's *Essay on Man* had been written in English, we added that. After these three titles, agreement became more difficult. As I recall, we soon enough added Frye's just-published *Anatomy of Criticism,* and perhaps Lewis' *The Allegory of Love* and maybe even Auerbach's *Mimesis*. To our chagrin, however, we were unable to achieve consensus on even so few as ten titles, and we submitted a list of only seven or eight. The brevity of the list—leaving aside whatever deficiencies in knowledge or judgment characterized our group—the brevity of the list was testimony both to the ephemerality of scholarly interpretation, on the one hand, and to the exceptional nature, on the other, of those few titles we salvaged.

Another previous act and conception with regard to *The Mirror and the Lamp* had occurred for me still earlier. In the summer of 1954, over a period of several weeks, I worked through the entire apparatus of footnotes in that volume, with extensive benefit to my own structures of learning. Even earlier, I had proudly come to the realization that Coleridge's metaphorical consciousness was a veritable jungle of plant imagery, only to find that before *The Mirror and the Lamp* appeared, Abrams had established this important and comprehensive truth in an article.

But the act of criticism itself, as opposed to these my praising pre-cogitations, must assume another structure. It must consider faults as well as merits, and in doing so it differs from the structure of interpretation. In fact, one of Coleridge's own prime critical maxims was phrased this way: "*until you understand a writer's ignorance, presume yourself ignorant of his understanding.*" In accordance with this principle, the twenty-second chapter of the *Biographia Literaria* is called "The characteristic defects of Wordsworth's poetry, with the principles from which the judgement, that they are defects, is deduced." Nor was this title in any way adventitious; for in his letters we have Coleridge's considered declaration that with regard to Wordsworth he "was convinced, that the detection of faults in his Poetry is indispensable to a rational appreciation of his Merits." Wordsworth, of course, did not much like any talk of defects, but then too his egotism was such that even praise was sometimes not enough. "He scorns even the admiration of himself," wrote Hazlitt, "thinking it a presumption in any one to suppose that he has taste or sense enough to understand him." Of the criticism in the *Biographia Literaria,* Henry Crabb Robinson reported that "Coleridge's book has given Wordsworth no pleasure.... With the criticism on the poetry too he is not satisfied. The praise is extravagant and the censure inconsiderate." Nevertheless, as Stephen Parrish has pointed out, Wordsworth did at the earliest opportunity alter his poetry to conform with Coleridge's criticisms.

Alteration, however, is not the real reason why identification of faults is essential to the process of criticism. It is rather that such negative consideration is necessary to establish the *contour* of the work that is placed in the canon: the process is something like running one's hands over a sculptured shape to know it more fully. More formally, Karl Popper has urged that the truth content of any theory should be measured not by the theory's verifiability but by its falsifiability. Only those theories that can be shown to be false in certain circumstances can be true in others; on the other hand, if a theory cannot be falsified, then it is nugatory and devoid of empirical content, as, for example, with medieval theories about the nature of angels. To extrapolate Popper's principle for our present purposes, we may say that to criticize a work adversely before its acceptance into the canon is not to correct it but to understand it more specifically.

I shall restrict myself to a single example of how the process of finding fault can make us better understand the contour of Abrams' work.

A Coleridgean Criticism of the Work of M. H. Abrams

In a review of *Natural Supernaturalism* in *The Yale Review* for Winter 1972—a review that originated as a tasting, but which I shall reinvoke as criticism on the threshold of canonicity—I took Abrams to task for imposing too simple a schematism on the varied materials with which he was concerned. "Abrams's categories," I said, "work well with Blake and Shelley, fairly well with Keats—or part of Keats—and not so well with Wordsworth. When applied to Coleridge, they result in judgments to which I find myself almost completely opposed." I now suggest that this reservation can apply to *The Mirror and the Lamp* as well. Just as Carlyle's elegant phrase "Natural Supernaturalism" did not entirely account for all the facts marshaled under its banner, so too does Yeats's striking and economical image of mirrors turning to lamps not entirely square with the facts it purports to organize.

Lamps are actually in short supply in Romantic imagery, while mirrors unfortunately abound, and in the most pivotal places. Shelley, in his *Defence of Poetry*, says—and Abrams takes note of the statement—that "poetry is a mirror which makes beautiful that which is distorted." Very well; we can accommodate an exception. But Wordsworth in the preface to *Lyrical Ballads*, a central theoretical document of Romanticism, says that "the Poet . . . considers man and nature as essentially adapted to each other, and the mind of man as naturally the mirror of the fairest and most interesting qualities of nature." Still more dismayingly, Friedrich Schlegel, in his *Athenäumsfragment 116*, another central theoretical statement of the Romantic sensibility, says that one of the characteristics of *romantische Poesie* is that "it alone can become, like the epic, a mirror of the whole circumambient world, an image of the age. And it can also, more than any other form, hover at the midpoint between the portrayed and the portrayer, free of all real and ideal self-interest, on the wings of poetic reflection, and can raise that reflection again and again to a higher power, can multiply it in an endless series of mirrors." Schlegel's "endless series of mirrors" finds a counterpart, yet again, in the "focusing mirror" of what is perhaps the most central document of French Romanticism. For Victor Hugo says, in his *Préface de Cromwell*, that "drama is the complete poetry": ". . . drama is a mirror where nature is reflected. But if this mirror be an ordinary mirror, a smooth and level surface, it will send back only a lusterless image of objects, without relief, an image faithful but without color; everyone knows that color and light are lost in a simple reflection. It is necessary, therefore, that drama be a focusing mirror that, far from weakening them, concentrates and condenses the coloring rays, that makes of a gleam a light, of a light a flame." Here, of course, the mirror takes on something of the function of what one might be pleased to call a lamp, though "lamp" is possibly too inert a word for Hugo's kinetic conception. Unfortunately, however, his mirror does not actually become a lamp, but remains precisely "un miroir de concentration."

To state the matter in brief, therefore, the attractive and aesthetically economical rubric of mirror and lamp begins to abrade and crumble under the onslaught of intractable facts. But if in this instance the attempt to falsify Abrams' theory might be thought to have succeeded, at the same time and in the same process of inspection it makes more clear for us a cardinal virtue of his technique, that is, his ability to unify very large heterogeneities of cultural fact and awareness under organizing ideas of unusual clarity and simplicity. There is something peculiarly satisfying about such rendering of diversity into simplicity; in truth, Coleridge defines beauty itself as multeity in unity, the seeing of the many in the one.

And if the faults of Abrams' procedure reveal its underlying elegance, merits inhere in his achievement far in excess of its faults. I shall note only two of them, and then conclude this paper with a quotation. The first of the merits to which I wish to call attention is that Abrams' work is not only massive statement but essential statement. No scholar can function in late-eighteenth- and early-nineteenth-century literature without using that work, becoming beholden to it, defining himself in terms of his reaction to it. The discussion of organism in *The Mirror and the Lamp*, for example, is still after a quarter of a century much the best and most revealing treatment of the topic that Oskar Walzel called the key to the Romantic view of the world.

Second, no other figure in English studies has ever produced two different and discrete interpretational syntheses of such magnitude as *The Mirror and the Lamp* and *Natural Supernaturalism*. Each in its own right is a landmark. Together they loom over the interpretational scene as decisively as the twin towers of the World Trade Center dominate the skyline of Manhattan.

So much for the explicit assessment of virtues and defects in Abrams' work. The future cultural disposition of that work with respect to canonicity is not yet clear. But what can be said at this juncture is that it constitutes an effort whose shape is large and whose weight is palpable, and as summarizing testimony to this present status I should like to offer, in concluding critical epitome, a second quotation from the same review from which I earlier quoted an adverse opinion of *Natural Supernaturalism:*

> Nonetheless, *Natural Supernaturalism* is an extraordinarily distinguished achievement. If I have felt it necessary to criticize certain aspects of this important and hugely learned work, it is because so vast a synthesis necessarily furnishes a greater area for disagreement than do lesser studies. Despite the reservations I have here suggested, the book seems to me correct in most of its major contentions. Its examination of Romantic attitudes is deep and satisfying, and in its command of its materials it recalls the monumental work of Rudolf Haym. I think it will unquestionably be seminal for many years to come. When one speaks of major work, this should be the kind of achievement that comes to mind.

The Genie in the Lamp:
M. H. Abrams and the
Motives of Literary History

LAWRENCE LIPKING

In Wellek's and Warren's influential *Theory of Literature* (1949), the chapter "Literary History" begins with a challenging question: "Is it *possible* to write literary history, that is, to write that which will be both literary and a history?" The answer, in 1949, was not at all clear; nor has it become much clearer in the last three decades. Despite the obvious fact that literary histories continue to be written, we still do not know whether they are possible—at least by absolute standards. In this respect literary histories resemble translations. From one point of view they seem inconceivably difficult—no one can reproduce the literary contexts and assumptions of another age any more than the texture and connotations of another language. But from another point of view they seem surprisingly easy; we rattle away in them all the time, like bilingual children, almost without noticing what we are doing. The practical difficulty comes between: in noticing what we are doing, yet still being able to do it. Self-conscious literary historians often develop a stutter.

There is good reason for stuttering. The demands of historical proof and demonstration conflict with the intuitive leaps of critical understanding; the attempt to define a *Zeitgeist* falters before the particularity and peculiarity of literary texts. Nor have many authors succeeded in practice. Most graduate students would be embarrassed, I suspect, if asked to name a single literary history earlier than the twentieth century. The genre is almost as unforgiving as time itself. Literary histories survive, if at all, as footnotes to the next literary history; evidence of the historical prejudices or fashions of an earlier age. While arguments about the possibility of literary history continue to swirl through the pages of such magazines as *New Literary History,* history conveys its own grim practical argument: old literary histories tend not to last. And very few indeed attain the status of classics.

Nevertheless, a few classics of literary history do survive. Whether or not we accept everything they say, they satisfy what Samuel Johnson called the only test that can be applied to works based not on scientific principles but on observation and experience: "length of duration and continuance of esteem." Johnson sets the term of literary merit at a century, the traditional period of incubation for a classic. But given the restlessness of modern times and the extreme fragility of literary history as a form, I think that we might consider any work classic that has endured and been esteemed for a quarter of a century. By this standard the work of M. H. Abrams, however we might want to criticize it, is already classical. *The Mirror and the Lamp* has survived its quarter century. Still fresh, it continues to be required reading for any literary historian; it continues to define the terms in which many people think. And like other classics, it can teach us a good deal about the problematics of its form: the practical difficulties, the practical solutions, of literary history.

For *The Mirror and the Lamp* and *Natural Supernaturalism,* one must emphasize, are very self-conscious books. Abrams' relatively unproblematical attitude toward texts—he still seems to believe, even in these deconstructed, radically indeterminate days, that texts contain meanings intended by authors and conveyed, more or less intelligibly, to readers—should not blind us to the complication and sophistication of his attitude toward his own materials. He does not begin his books with the year one, or the year 1798, but with the chaos of critical theories or with the labyrinthine relations between a poem and the spirit of the age. The circuitous Romantic journey of *Natural Supernaturalism*, which bends back on itself to end with the same passage from Wordsworth where it began, emblemizes Abrams' view of history: less a chronological sequence than a circular and multilayered pattern of understanding. His discourse does not obey simple laws of cause and effect; it is shaped self-consciously by art. It traffics in "orientations"; "metaphors"; "designs." Like many classics, that is to say, Abrams' classics of literary history are partly reflexive; they comment on their own mode of operation and reasons for being. As *Hamlet* may be considered a classic revenge play not so much because it slavishly observes the stage conventions as because it takes those conventions—the problematic nature of delay and retribution—as a part of its subject, so *The Mirror and the Lamp* is a classic because it explores, at least to some extent, the difficulties inherent in the nature of literary history.

Let me be more specific. The reason that Abrams' books seem so central to the enterprise of literary history, and are read by so many students and scholars whose work lies outside the Romantic period, is that Abrams supplies some of the best answers currently available to certain perennial questions. How do we define the essence of a literary period? What is the relationship between continuity and change in poetic art? How do critical ideas become realized in works of imagination? And even: Is it *possible* to write literary history? Most literary historians take these questions for granted. Abrams does not. His arguments become most searching exactly at the point where the field itself becomes most problematical: the assumptions, only half formulated, that shape the questions we ask and the models we construct. Why are we doing what we are doing? Most of us, as scholars, do not quite know; but we like to think that *someone* knows. If we rubbed the lamp a genie would pop out: someone who could justify, if he had to, the assumptions behind our work as well as his own. For many literary historians, Abrams is that someone.

What *are* the motives, then, for literary history? A survey of Abrams' assumptions might well begin with a long look at two full titles: *The Mirror and the Lamp: Romantic Theory and the Critical Tradition;* and *Natural Supernaturalism: Tradition and Revolution in Romantic Literature.* Both titles are rich as well as catchy; and they have the virtue, all too rare in their emblematic genre, of telling us a good deal about the insides of the books. But both are Janus-faced. They look before and after, suggesting a sequence in which expressive lamps replace mimetic mirrors and the imagination naturalizes the supernatural. Yet further inspection reveals that the two icons depend less on sequence than on paradox: the moment when mirror and lamp, supernature and nature, interpenetrate and become one. (The first book takes its title from Yeats's prayer that "the mirror turn lamp," the second from Carlyle's desire "to exhibit the Wonder of daily life and common things" in a perpetual "Natural Supernaturalism." Opposites attract.) Hence each title pits a ballast of "tradition" against a radical Romantic challenge to that tradition, yet implies a variety of possible results: a break, a synthesis, or even both at once in an "apocalyptic marriage." Backward and forward, systole and diastole. On more than one occasion Abrams has spoken of another, yet unwritten version of Romantic history, a version that would give the center stage to Byronic irony. I cannot predict what title that history might have—many of the obvious oppositions, like Fallen Angel or The Sea and the Prison, seem rather too melodramatic—but the subtitle comes readily enough to mind: Romantic Tradition and the Ironic Countervoice. To my ears it sounds like a classic.

The peculiar authority of Abrams' books does not derive from any formula, however, but from their confrontation with a central issue of literary history: the search for a moment when everything changed. Most of the great literary histories share the same interest. They tell a story of two worlds. One world—the old world, the world we have lost—obeys the laws of hierarchy, order, decorum, continuity, and faith; its art tends to be "naive" (in Schiller's sense), mimetic, and unself-conscious. The other world—the modern world, the world after the fall, our world—is characterized by individualism, private emotion, discontinuity, and antinomianism; its art tends to be "sentimental" and self-consciously original. And the change from one world to the other is irreversible—except in the work of certain literary historians, who recreate the old world, through an act of learned sympathy, expressly for the purpose of showing how much it has changed. Before and after; the Janus face. The focus on a revolution in consciousness, which Abrams makes explicit, supplies many other scholars with an implicit theme. We look to the past and its writings to define their strangeness; all that they are, and all that we are not. And it is because Abrams deals so directly with this theme, allowing it to rise to the surface, that his work seems so central. He probes the concern at the heart of literary history: the sense of change.

Yet why should this concern be so prominent? Do we narrow our literary histories too much by focusing so intently on a moment of change? Surely the effect can be distorting. A few years ago a bright undergraduate who had heard my introductory lectures on the eighteenth century, the Romantic poets, and modern poetry commented that, though he liked them all very much, one ever so tiny reservation had occurred: all of them were the same. And perhaps he was right. Each of them had started with a picture of a conservative older literary world, and had gone on to show that within a few years everything had changed. The downfall of the old order! Revolution and crisis! The breaking of the circle! The rise of the middle class! From the closed world to the infinite universe! The dissociation of sensibility! The apocalypse of World War I! The mirror and the lamp! I felt lucky, in fact, that he had not heard my lectures on the fathers of the church or on the Renaissance—two more versions, doubtless, of exactly the same old story. And if I were required to give those lectures once again, there would probably be no difference. What other story exists, after all, but the story of tradition and revolution? At least for those of us who are typical literary historians.

No one has told this story better than Abrams—more fully, more deeply. Indeed, his efforts, along with those of many other gifted Romantic scholars, have helped to make the Romantic movement a focal point—perhaps *the* focal point—for literary history. Though many other lines can be drawn between "before" and "after," the moment when everything changed, though almost every period between the fifth century B.C. and the 1960s has been proposed as a candidate, Romanticism now seems our best model (I prefer not to call it the best *paradigm*) for the structure of literary revolutions. This view of Romanticism exists on every level, from the most sophisticated scholar to the most casual student. Sometimes it appears that babes in arms, scarcely past their nursery rhymes, command one fact of literary history: that something called "Neoclassicism" was succeeded by something called "Romanticism." Nor should one underestimate the power of this formulation. I know from grim experience that no suppression of that creeping word "Neoclassicism" will prevent it from springing up again like the hydra on the final examination; and though only one of my lectures administers a dose of pure, unadulterated Abrams (the Wordsworthian pattern of paradise, fall, and redemption), that is the lecture that my students tend to carry away with them.

Merely because a view is commonplace, popular, and orthodox, we are not required to conclude, of course, that it must be untrue. But certainly the success of Abrams' way of looking at Romanticism has brought some disquietude in its wake. Nor do we lack ironic countervoices. Eighteenth-century scholars enjoy pointing to the many lamps in their period, and Romantic scholars to the many mirrors in theirs; the Romantic hope of redemption through the imagination can itself be castigated as a dangerous illusion, a fall from grace. The power of Abrams' tightly woven emblems has occasioned a whole unraveling industry, dedicated to showing how much in Romanticism evades his schema. Everyone likes to attack an orthodoxy.

Yet Abrams' work has survived its critics, and continues to furnish the standard. He is far too scrupulous a scholar, far too thoughtful a historian of ideas, to vulgarize or falsify his account of literary change. Moreover, his books do full justice to the continuities that give meaning to change. I have said that the story of before and after provides a basis for most literary history; but an older impulse, equally strong, searches out influences and precedents, as if to demonstrate that every thought depends on an earlier thought and nothing ever really changes. *Plus ça change* . . . , or the law of conservation of ideas. You will find it, I always feel safe in telling my students, somewhere in Quintilian. Abrams knows Quintilian. A deeply conservative temperament, he never fails to remind us that the seeds of Romanticism are planted in the lowest stratum of antiquity. No books on the Romantic poets explore their traditions further or wider. That is how *The Mirror and the Lamp* and *Natural Supernaturalism* earn the right to define the point of change. And for all its emphasis on revolution, in the last analysis Abrams' work is profoundly comforting. Even at the moment when everything changed, he tells us, the change was following those purposes laid down by history, and conserving the best of the past. The mirror can turn lamp while retaining its best qualities as mirror; the wonder of the supernatural, far from being dispersed by the Enlightenment, can be naturalized into "a simple produce of the common day." Abrams does not ratify a divorce; he celebrates a wedding.

Nevertheless, the organization of literary history around moments of change, the before and after in human consciousness, has some disturbing consequences. Teleology and avant-

gardism preoccupy too many scholars; gazing ahead and behind, we often stumble or stamp on the poem under our feet. To
narrow the problems to a single question: Is it possible, will it
ever be possible, for Romantic scholars to give fair play to the
eighteenth century? At one time we conjured up a period called
Pre-Romanticism, whose poets were described as embryos or
primitive stages of the coming revolution; natural children who
evolved, in the nick of time, into Wordsworth. But that view at
least required an occasional glance at the poets in question. The
more recent fashion of considering Romantic poetry a direct
response to Milton manages to avoid that inconvenience by
finessing the eighteenth century entirely. When Milton dropped
from heaven into Blake's left foot he did not have to pass, apparently, through the heads of Pope or Cowper. The tradition
continues. With a few notable exceptions (such as Abrams and
Geoffrey Hartman), Romantic scholars tend to be complacently
ignorant of eighteenth-century poetry. A reference to a rape
and an elegy, some generalizations about science, the great chain
of being, and graveyards, a few words like Wit, Nature, Imagination, and Genius coupled to verses without benefit of *OED*, usually exhaust the stock. Evidently the glamour of change counts
for a good deal more than knowledge of what poetry was like
before. The punishment in such cases, fortunately, exactly fits the
crime: all Romanticists who commit a solecism about
eighteenth-century poetry should be condemned to a year's
hard study of James Thomson (not to be let off even for *Liberty*).
Wordsworth's own sketch of the history of English poetry, you
will recall, allows Thomson twice the space of Milton.

The tendency of Romantic scholars to define their period by
rejecting or misrepresenting the previous period is not, of
course, unique. Most periods begin that way. The Renaissance
invented itself by inventing the myth of the Dark preceding
Ages; the Enlightenment improved on that periodization by ac-
cusing the Renaissance itself of superstition and credulity; and
one problem in periodizing the writers of today is that, unlike

the classic Moderns, we no longer have the Victorian Age to kick around. Rejection is what fathers are for. Nor, in the interests of fairness, should I omit a balancing question: Will it ever be possible for eighteenth-century scholars to be fair to the Romantics? While the division of literature into before and after confers a certain progressive or teleological luster on the after, it also lends a pleasant aura of resistance and nostalgia to the before. If the caricature of the eighteenth century as a time of tranquillity and order was designed to serve Romantic interests, many eighteenth-century scholars still guard it as they would guard their lives. Après moi le déluge! Wordsworth, Coleridge, Shelley, and Keats often misrepresented the standards of the eighteenth century; the reviewers, trained in eighteenth-century standards, often misrepresented the poetry of Wordsworth, Coleridge, Shelley, and Keats. Surely both sides got exactly what they deserved. Periods begin with manifestos, clearing a space for change; no wonder, then, that literary historians spend so much of their time studying manifestos.

Periods, that is to say, consolidate around the residue of yesterday's arguments. Yet why should yesterday's arguments concern us? Should not a scholar, if anyone, remain aloof from taking sides? Almost every historical scholar has questioned, at some point in his life, the usefulness of period labels and definitions of the *Zeitgeist* and periodization itself. Why must we think in periods? Too often they represent not even yesterday's arguments, but only yesterday's rumors. And too much of the truth slips through the mesh.

Consider, for instance, one of the best-kept secrets of literary history. What was the most innovative decade in English literature? Many plausible answers are likely to spring to mind: the 1590s, of course, and the 1790s, and perhaps the 1910s or 1920s. No conclusive proof can be offered, naturally, to demonstrate the correctness of one answer or another. But allow me to suggest a decade that probably does *not* spring to many minds: the 1740s; or more precisely, the ten years that followed the fall of Walpole in 1742. Two incomparable works of art may be said to usher in the period: Handel's *Messiah* (1742) and Hogarth's *Marriage à la Mode* (1743-45). In prose fiction the decade witnessed the most significant of all modern literary innovations, the rise of the novel in the hands of Richardson, Fielding, and Smollett. In poetry it brought forth the *New Dunciad*, the fully revised *Seasons* and the *Castle of Indolence, The Vanity of Human Wishes*, the best work of Collins and Gray, the fits and starts of Akenside and the Wartons, and (most influential of all) the night thoughts of Young and Blair. But the full richness of the decade cannot be appreciated without consideration of its intellectual prose. Johnson, in his boldest creative period, produced most of the first substantial English dictionary and distilled his prose style into the pure wine of *The Rambler*. British philosophy reached its high-water mark with Hume's enquiries into human understanding (1748) and the principles of morals (1751), Hartley's *Observations on Man* (1749), and Berkeley's peculiar "chain of philosophical reflections," *Siris* (1744). Bolingbroke's *Letters on the Study of History* (1752) set off the greatest age of British history writing. And more modest forms, such as letters and memoirs, flourished as never before. What decade has ever given rise to so many originals? Ladies and gentlemen: I give you the 1740s.

Subtract something, if you like, for exaggeration. The question remains: Why has the innovative spirit of the 1740s received so little publicity even in the best literary histories? A full answer would have to explore many issues for which space is lacking— for instance, the modern redefinition of "literature," which has eased intellectual prose out of the canon or banished it to the nebulous outer space of "nonfiction"; and our tendency to arrange history according to centuries, so that major changes are scheduled to arrive conveniently in the nineties, seldom in the mids. But a partial answer might focus on three conditions. First, the 1740s was *too* innovative a decade. So many different works originated, of so many different literary kinds, that the new possibilities required time to be absorbed and exploited. For example, *fifty years later* Wordsworth and Coleridge could still regard Collins as a neglected poet of the avant-garde and Hartley as a philosopher whose time was yet to come. One great consolidating poet often has more of an impact, in defining a period, than a host of minor originals. Second, the writers of the 1740s succeeded better at creating works of art than at issuing manifestos. Fielding's preface to *Joseph Andrews,* Johnson's "Drury-Lane Prologue" and "Plan of a Dictionary," the Wartons' attacks on Pope, all look to the past as much as the future. Their claims are less radical than the work they introduce, and even at the moment of innovation (as in Fielding's recipe for the "comic epic-poem in prose") they conciliate and conserve. (Compare the public relations of several movements in the twentieth century, whose manifestos often convey an excitement and urgency missing in the art.) Literary historians, as lazy as the public, require some prodding to notice the new.

Yet a third reason may be still more important. If the innovations of the 1740s have yet to make their full impact on literary history, the crucial obstacle may well be that they seldom claim to go beyond literature itself, to effect a transformation of *mind.* Revolutions in forms, even revolutions in ideas, do not necessarily mark the beginning of a new era. What does seem necessary is a change in the state of mind. Once literary historians have been convinced of that, and not until then, they will declare an old period over, a new period begun. Clearly works of art changed in the 1740s; it is not so clear that metaphors of mind went through a similar change. And partly for that reason 1798, not 1742, is the date that every schoolboy knows.

Let me return to *The Mirror and the Lamp.* If any one passage can be called a summary of so rich and complex a book, it is probably this one:

> In any period, the theory of mind and the theory of art tend to be
> integrally related and to turn upon similar analogues, explicit or

submerged. To put the matter schematically: for the representative eighteenth-century critic, the perceiving mind was a reflector
of the external world; the inventive process consisted in a reassem-
bly of 'ideas' which were literally images, or replicas of sensations;
and the resulting art work was itself comparable to a mirror pre-
senting a selected and ordered image of life. By substituting a
projective and creative mind and, consonantly, an expressive and
creative theory of art, various romantic critics reversed the basic
orientation of all aesthetic philosophy. [P. 69]

This is a powerful and persuasive statement. It can be substantiated, as Abrams has substantiated it, with copious quotations
from Romantic theorists. Indeed, so much evidence supports
the argument that it appears almost like second nature—if not
utterly convincing, then at least as convincing as any generaliza-
tion about the movement of ideas in history could hope to be.
Yet I cannot help wondering about the *status* of the argument. It
depends on a chain of analogues, not only between the theory of
mind and the theory of art but between a theory of perception
and a theory of creation, as well as between ideas and metaphors
or "orientations." And then, even granting the validity of these
analogues, we must suspend our disbelief in another implicit
analogue, between the orientation of aesthetic philosophy and
the essence of works of art. This analogue becomes still more
prevalent in *Natural Supernaturalism,* whose eloquent analyses of
poems constantly suggest a shaping set of ideological assumptions, if not actually a sort of world soul that inspires the poet
with the mind of his age. Philosophers have a right to debate
such assumptions, of course; but what have they to do with the
writing of poems? If the mind of an age is analogous to a human
mind, shall we compare the Romantic period with the mind of
Kant, so determined to pursue his ideas to their conclusions, or
with the mind of Goethe, so rich in inconsistencies, whose poems
furnish philosophy with its raw materials but never descend into
philosophy itself?

Analogy and metaphor inform all of Abrams' work. Indeed, if

I were to compare his books with a single great predecessor, I should point to Bishop Butler's famous *Analogy of Religion* (1736). Both men accept analogy, not as conclusive evidence, but as probable evidence that offers a guide to life; both men are reverent toward creation. While Butler never underestimates the difficulty of understanding God through the evidences of Nature—he argues strongly, in fact, that Nature cannot replace Revelation as the basis of religion—he patiently combs the text before him, the universe as we know it, in order to find the universal intelligence that has created it. Abrams also seeks a mind. With some of Butler's "somber gravity," his "unusual power of looking dispassionately at the facts, and reporting upon them without distortion" (in the words of Basil Willey), he reads criticism and poetry as if they were the voice of a mighty collective purpose—even a revelation.

Hence *Natural Supernaturalism*, still more than *The Mirror and the Lamp*, often balances between the methods of religion and the methods of science. The title itself might be read (in Carlyle as well as Abrams) as analogous to the eighteenth-century phrases for scientific investigation: "natural philosophy" and "natural religion." I have said that Abrams views texts as relatively unproblematical; but all his students will remember the moments when his patient explication of poems yields to a finer tone, a reverent and rapt communion with the poem that stirs some students with wonder and alarm, as if they might have to pluck his sleeve to hold him on the earth. Such moments are precious; they indicate Abrams' glimpse, within the poem, of a purpose, a design, a mind—something to worship. The lamp of the mind is consecrated; sometimes, rubbed the right way, it reveals a genie. The literary histories of Abrams contain within them the shadow of a secular scripture: the analogy of poetic texts to a universal creative intelligence.

Literary historians could hardly request a nobler justification of what they do. Abrams seems to unfold the meaning, not merely of individual poems, but of the greater history to which each poem contributes; what Shelley called "that great poem, which all poets, like the co-operating thoughts of one great mind, have built up since the beginning of the world." Literary historians, like poets themselves, can hope to join the thoughts of that one mind. Nor should we forget the deep pleasure, the high poetic pleasure, of perceiving that a period has a soul—

> While with an eye made quiet by the power
> Of harmony, and the deep power of joy,
> We see into the life of things.
> [*Tintern Abbey*, ll. 47–49]

Abrams, like Wordsworth, casts a spell.

Yet the analogy of poetic texts, like the analogy of religion, is not without its dangers. Fifteen years after Butler's *Analogy*, near the end of my innovative decade, David Hume produced what many readers still consider the ultimate refutation of the argument from design: *Dialogues concerning Natural Religion*. Is there a mind behind nature? If so, says Philo, it is a mind we shall never comprehend. "When the coherence of the parts of a stone, or even that composition of parts, which renders it extended; when these familiar objects, I say, are so inexplicable, and contain circumstances so repugnant and contradictory; with what assurance can we decide concerning the origin of worlds, or trace their history from eternity to eternity?" Both Demea and Cleanthes smile at those words; Demea, because like Bishop Butler he considers the incomprehensible contradictions of nature a friend to revelation; but Cleanthes, because he perceives "some raillery or artificial malice." Abrams, I suspect, might side with Cleanthes. He understands the problems of an argument from analogy; he knows that one can never *prove* causation, the existence of a particular *Zeitgeist* or a *primum mobile*. But neither will he concede that poems, like stones, must remain essentially incoherent and inexplicable in the absence of revelation. The design of poems, the purposeful coherence of aesthetic thought, argue for a mind behind them—a mind that can be comprehended by anyone willing to use his own. Undogmatically but firmly his books stand by that analogy. What other kind of literary history can we conceive? Philo will not help us much here; except by suggesting, like some more recent literary historians, an abandonment to the analogical process, with a frank acknowledgment that no analogy carries any more authority than another, that the mind we perceive in texts always turns into a reflection of our own, and that every version of history involves, in the last analysis, an intrinsic element of the personal and the arbitrary. Already literary histories based on such principles have begun to appear, though not without animadversions from such critics as Cleanthes. "The total infirmity of human reason, the absolute incomprehensibility of the Divine Nature, the great and universal misery and still greater wickedness of men; these are strange topics surely to be so fondly cherished by orthodox divines and doctors." Doctors of literature who cherish the absolute incomprehensibility of texts may encounter difficulty in ascribing any purpose to literary history—or retaining the faith of the common reader.

More modestly, however, literary history might be conceived without reference to analogy, as that strict "history of literature as an art" that Wellek and Warren once thought might just make literary history possible. Detaching poems from the world spirit, we begin to see them in a different way: as a series of works of art linked by nothing more universal than the response of one artist to another, or an almost infinite number of variations on a set of conventions, genres, styles, words, images, ideas, forms, and melodies. Above all we can try to see each poem as itself, rather than as an example of something else. Abrams himself, in his role of general editor of *The Norton Anthology of English Literature,* furnishes a model of this limited historical purpose, supplying just the proper amount of information about each poem without striving to relate it to a larger scheme. The task of annotation enforces some measure of discretion and discipline; many literary historians could profit from it. When we read "Kubla Khan," for instance, we do need to envisage it as an emanation of the Romantic Mind? The nightmare spawned by a sleep of reason? the harbinger of a great new wave of consciousness sweeping Europe? a compressed version of an epic on the fall of Jerusalem (as E. S. Shaffer has brilliantly argued), applying the principles of Higher Criticism to the nature of poetic inspiration? Or would we do better as literary historians to restrict ourselves (in the manner of art historians) to matters of precedent and craft: the stock of images in Coleridge's reading, the immediate circumstances of composition, the genre of reverie, or the obsessive set of rhythms (half remembered, I believe, from Collins' "Ode on the Poetical Character")? Could we not usefully spend less time on the significance and more on the style?

Perhaps we could. The first sketches of English literary history, jotted down by such poets as Pope and Gray, assumed that a historian must begin by arranging his subject into schools: groups of poets associated, not through a common mind, but through a common technique. Those sketches have never been followed to an end. Despite a few brave but inconclusive efforts by literary historians (for example, Josephine Miles, Donald Davie, Alastair Fowler), usually poets themselves, the history of poetic schools and poetic technique remains a long way from being written. But even the best such history, I suspect, would not supplant Abrams' in power or popularity. For the need to discern a mind and purpose in literary history goes far beyond scholarly curiosity or a concern for accurate detail. It touches upon our own intimate relations with literature; our need to sense, in the process of literary change, in its radical advances and slow declines, something like a life.

The motive that I am suggesting is hardly one that could be demonstrated by a series of arguments. But perhaps it can be sketched impressionistically, by attending to matters of texture and feeling. In the work of every great literary historian with whom I am acquainted, a certain note eventually begins to sound and swell and reverberate. It occurs even in the earliest historians, such as Thomas Warton, Girolamo Tiraboschi, or the Abbé Goujet. It echoes and resonates through the work of Taine, Saintsbury, De Sanctis, Lovejoy. The great continental literary historians of our own century, such as Auerbach and Curtius, also sound it. And to speak more personally—whenever I have heard a mature literary historian express his deepest concerns, I have recognized the same note at last, and have come to wait for it and vibrate to it like an old friend.

Of what note am I speaking? Nothing more mysterious than the ground of sadness that accompanies almost any representation of a decisive and irreversible change in human consciousness. "A time there was..." From Goldsmith through Wordsworth, Coleridge, and Byron to Hardy, the phrase implies a loss that cannot be restored. Literary historians repeat it; literary critics do not. The authors of manifestos, the most fashionable literary critics, often tend to sound a joyous optimistic note. Up till now, as T. S. Eliot said in *The Sacred Wood* and I. A. Richards in *Principles of Literary Criticism* and the Marxists in the thirties and the New Critics in the forties and Northrop Frye in the fifties and the structuralists in the sixties and the various metacritics in the seventies, up till now there has been almost no criticism worthy of the name. But the time has come. *We are on the verge.* The future belongs to us. And soon, if only we forget the mistakes of the past, a new and better criticism will begin.

Literary historians are seldom privileged to sound that note. Most of them are in love with the past, or at least with a few moments in it. A time there was, and bliss was it in that dawn to be alive.... What Abrams conveys about the Romantic period, certainly, is not just a point of view but his own sympathy and love. Literary historians live in two worlds: one through the accident of birth and one through choice. Yet the world they have chosen is always receding. The faery way of writing, Thomas Warton knew, had long been over; the Renaissance would come no more, for De Sanctis or Italy; even the ability to read the classics, Curtius suspected, was vanishing fast, and now there were no more classics. When a great literary historian reaches this point, usually toward the end of the last in a series of lectures, a hush falls over the room; his words echo into the silence like the pang of a great string breaking. For literary history deals with something that has gone: a private interior possession kept alive only so long as disciples can be found to carry it on. The past is fragile. It is not an accident, I think, that so many of the best literary historians have flourished at times when civilization itself seemed to be ending—Germany in the thirties is a striking instance. The story of change carries within it the principle of entropy and dissolution. The nightingale of Clio flies at midnight.

If the field of the literary historian provides him with the materials of an elegy, moreover, he can also observe the pattern of one particular history closer at hand: the story of his life. It is Curtius you mourn for. The note of sadness acquires a special poignancy, in one literary history after another, through association with the life of the author. Civilizations are preserved, after all, through innumerable acts of sympathy, in the individual minds that harbor and recreate them; the decline, the coming dissolution of any one of those minds prefigures the passing of a ripe interior civilization. Mourning for classical antiquity, for the waning of the Middle Ages, for the concept of sincerity, for the world of nature, literary historians cannot help touching on themselves. One story keeps recurring: a time there was. Once the world was young—and then the darkness came.

Sometimes this note sounds too obtrusively, and then it seems merely sentimental. But in the best literary historians the relationship between the lost civilization they describe and the interior civilization they exemplify can be woven with subtle and delicate strands. Consider, for one last time, the work of Abrams. In one respect, the period he has chosen and his own attitude toward it supply a counterpoint to the note I have traced. For the

Romantic poets, as he describes them, are redemptive. The final section of *The Mirror and the Lamp* is called "The Use of Romantic Poetry," and it transmits not only a historical phenomenon—the way in which the quasi-religious romantic view of the poet provided the Victorians with a means of justifying and defending the art—but a permanent state of mind. Abrams does not quite suggest that a proper understanding of Romantic poets can also redeem *us*. But the generosity of his perspective, his ability to recover a reverence toward nature and the mind in the face of modern discontinuities, inspires a considerable optimism. It is not too late, he seems to say, to become a member of this civilization—to take it in. Nor does his defense of Romanticism rely, like so many other literary histories, on hostility toward the alternatives. He summarizes the issues calmly, without animus, and encourages us to make our own choice. The optimism is infectious. *The Mirror and the Lamp* exhibits the virtues of Romantic doctrine: a seriousness and a possibility of redemption that continue to hold out hope.

In *Natural Supernaturalism* the argument about redemption has become more open and more troubled. The elegiac note begins to prevail. "A number of our writers and artists have turned away, in revulsion or despair, not only from the culture of Western humanism but from the biological conditions of life itself, and from all life-affirming values" (p. 445). At the very end of the book Abrams returns to the documents of "The Use of Poetry," Shelley's and Wordsworth's defenses of poetry; but now the concluding words are darker. "If such affirmations strike a contemporary ear as deluded or outworn, that may be the index of their relevance to an age of profounder dereliction and dismay than Shelley and Wordsworth knew" (p. 462). We should not overstate the marks of dismay in this passage; *Natural Supernaturalism* cannot be reduced to a formula of Romantic salvation and modern damnation, or expulsion from the garden. Indeed, Abrams' sensitive response to a wide range of literature, and his sympathy with postromantic problems, are exactly what earns him the right to a final judgment. Yet redemption seems very far off, at the end, and very precarious. If we complete the book in the way that seems intended, by rereading Wordsworth's "Prospectus" once again with a new knowledge and understanding gained from the book as a whole, the poem acquires a new weight and poignance—more lovely, deeper than before, but receding into old hopes and comforts whose beauty depends on the sense of ending.

Why is there so much satisfaction in that ending? One possible answer cannot be omitted: perhaps Abrams, like most of his fellow literary historians, is *right* when he deplores the dereliction of contemporary life. Perhaps things really are falling apart, and universal darkness does cover all. (Even young people today happily endorse this theory.) But another answer also deserves a hearing. The literary historian, I have said, lives in two worlds. Yet in the best literary histories the two worlds join. Imaginatively realized, the past becomes usable; it lives again in the example of the historian and his work. Again and again the great literary historians, like the best poets, discover that the shaping intention of history as a whole resembles a mind like their own. Thus Wordsworth, in the prophetic moment of his prospectus, discerns in universal history a curiously familiar face:

> —And if with this
> I mix more lowly matter; with the thing
> Contemplated, describe the Mind and Man
> Contemplating; and who, and what he was,
> The transitory Being that beheld
> This Vision,—when and where, and how he lived;—
> Be not this labour useless. If such theme
> May sort with highest objects, then, dread Power,
> Whose gracious favour is the primal source
> Of all illumination, may my Life
> Express the image of a better time. . . .
> ["Prospectus," ll. 93–103]

Abrams holds out a similar hope. His books, and his own benevolent presence within them, express the image of a better
time: not only the time of the Romantics, but the time of a true
meeting of minds. The mind of history, the mind of the poet,
the mind of the reader, all come together, within his work, in
mutual illumination. And all are kindled, of course, by the mind
of the literary historian, the maker and the guardian of the
flame. That is the genie in the lamp.

The Mirror Stage

JONATHAN CULLER

The Mirror and the Lamp is now such a classic that it is easy to forget the peculiar power it had for many readers in its first decade. Those of us who had been nurtured on the New Criticism and thought Donne and the moderns the supreme examples of poetic achievement were inclined to find Romantic poetry the aberration of an age and sensibility out of tune with our own. The Romantics, we had heard, thought poetry a spontaneous overflow of feeling rather than a verbal construct, an expression of personality rather than an impersonal and comprehensively ironic form. We needed precisely such a guide as *The Mirror and the Lamp,* which would judiciously explain Romantic theory, enabling us to grasp its relation to other theories of poetry and to see Romantic literature as a comprehensible historical phenomenon. We thus came to read Romantic poetry as a reflection of the projects Abrams had described: expression rather than imitation, and "an attempt to overcome . . . the cleavage between subject and object, between the vital, purposeful, value-full world of private experience and the dead postulated world of extension, quantity, and motion."[1]

The material in this chapter appears, in different form, in my book *The Pursuit of Signs,* published by Routledge & Kegan Paul Ltd. and Cornell University Press, copyright © 1981 by Jonathan Culler.

[1]M. H. Abrams, *The Mirror and the Lamp* (New York: Oxford University Press,

The Mirror and the Lamp became the glass in which we saw Romanticism, but it also, unexpectedly, claimed to show us ourselves. Seeking to understand the assumptions of a literary tradition very different from the one we prized, we turned to it for enlightenment about a historical past. Imagine our bewilderment at its opening sentence: "The development of literary theory in the lifetime of Coleridge was to a surprising extent the making of the modern critical mind." Much of the power of *The Mirror and the Lamp* came from its demonstration that a whole series of contemporary critical concepts, including those that one had thought of as antiromantic, had in fact been formulated by Coleridge and other Romantic critics: the notion of the poem as heterocosm or self-contained universe, which must display organic unity and achieve the resolution of contraries; the conception of organic form and the inseparability of form and content; and finally the conception of good poetry as the product of a unified sensibility or imagination that fused together thought and feeling—in general, the notion that a poem must not mean but be.

In identifying the romantic sources of current critical notions *The Mirror and the Lamp* did indeed serve as a mirror: we looked into it and saw ourselves. It thus inaugurated what psychoanalysis calls the mirror stage, in which the child discovers his "self" by identifying with the image he perceives in a mirror.[2] The other that he sees in a mirror and can grasp as a totality turns out to be himself; thus the constitution of the self is dependent on the perception of the self as other. *The Mirror and the Lamp,* in describing romantic theory, became a mirror in which the contemporary critic could discover who and what he was. Various notions one had picked up here and there, various interpretive operations one was accustomed to perform, as-

---

1953), p. 65: Hereafter quotations from this work will be identified by page numbers in the text.

[2]For discussion see Jacques Lacan, "Le stade du miroir comme formateur de la fonction du Je," in *Ecrits* (Paris: Seuil, 1966), pp. 93–100.

sumptions of which one may have been unaware, were here explicitly integrated, shown to cohere in a totality. Through this image of the other, this specular representation, the budding critic discovered that he or she had a theory of literature. Such specularity carries with it certain dangers. When the mother of Narcissus, the nymph Liriope, asks Tiresias whether her son will live to an old age, the blind seer replies, "If he never recognizes himself." Narcissus' initial failure to recognize his reflection in the pool fueled an illusory hope, but when he did recognize himself there, this brought a graver dilemma. To look in the mirror and discover that one is a Romantic, when one had thought one was antiromantic or, at the very least, postromantic, is not the most pleasing of fates, but it seems to be an unavoidable mirror stage. Not to recognize ourselves in the image that appears in *The Mirror and the Lamp* would be a wishful error, like Narcissus' failure to recognize himself. But to recognize ourselves in *The Mirror and the Lamp* brings cold comfort.

Cold comfort, because to look into the mirror with a good lamp, to see the self as other, is to inaugurate the complex specular play of identification and alienation. The account of romantic critical principles in *The Mirror and the Lamp* initiates a critique of modern critical principles by showing us the self as other. In particular, these historical analyses reveal critical theory as an economy of metaphors. Consider the notion of organic form—linchpin, as it were, of the New Criticism—which more than any other concept regulates our analysis of poems. Here is *The Mirror and the Lamp* on Coleridge:

> It is astonishing how much of Coleridge's critical writing is couched in terms that are metaphorical for art and literal for a plant; if Plato's dialectic is a wilderness of mirrors, Coleridge's is a very jungle of vegetation. Only let the vehicles of his metaphors come alive, and you see all the objects of criticism writhe surrealistically into plants or parts of plants, growing in tropical profusion. Authors, characters, poetic genres, poetic passages, words, meter, logic become seeds, trees, flowers, blossoms, fruit, bark, and sap. [P. 169]

This passage, of course, is having some fun at the expense of Coleridge and the succeeding critics who have adopted his plants, but it is also extremely astute: "only let the vehicles of his metaphors come alive," Abrams says. This is what is at issue here, the "life" of language and figure. Coleridge's organic language insists that poems, "the objects of criticism," are not the lifeless products of fancy, dead figures, mechanical contrivances, but the living products of imagination, language with a life of its own. But a language come alive, as Abrams suggests, is a language unable to control its own tropology, writhing surrealistically "in tropical profusion." Though Abrams may be poking fun at Coleridge for his metaphors, his own language shows that Coleridge has a point, that language can lead a life of its own, even run wild. Planted in Abrams' lively language is a plant effect, a tropism, a tropical profusion; the pun on tropes and tropics might even count as mild "surrealistic writhing."

This passage can be treated as the beginning of what we now call a deconstructive reading of organicist theory: the revelation of a self-deconstructive movement within Romantic theoretical discourse, whose major insights are aporias revealed by the very attempt to conceal them. *The Mirror and the Lamp* helps us to follow this movement in Romantic theory by illuminating what Jacques Derrida calls the structured genealogy of certain key figures and distinctions, showing how an opposition on which the theory relies subverts itself in the course of theoretical argument.[3]

A central distinction contrasts mechanism with organicism and proposes, as Abrams says, "the replacement of a mechanical

[3]Jacques Derrida, *Positions* (Paris: Minuit, 1972), p. 15. For deconstructive readings of Romantic theory, see Derrida's "Economimesis," in Sylviane Agacinski et al., *Mimesis des articulations* (Paris: Aubier-Flammarion, 1975), pp. 55–93. Among deconstructive readings of romantic literature are Paul de Man, *Allegories of Reading* (New Haven: Yale University Press, 1979), pt. 2; Cynthia Chase, "The Accidents of Disfiguration: Literal and Rhetorical Readings in Book V of *The Prelude*," *Studies in Romanticism*, 18 (Winter 1979), 547–65; and Richard Rand, "Geraldine," *Glyph*, 3 (1978), 74–97.

process by a living plant as the implicit paradigm governing the description of the process and product of literary invention" (p. 158). This replacement distinguishes the freedom and creativity of the poetic imagination from the mechanical processes of fancy. Fancy operates according to mechanistic principles of associationist psychology; it is determined; it cannot originate but only combine. Imagination, on the other hand, is essentially vital, undetermined, and originary; it exercises a creative freedom like the freedom of God: "a repetition in the finite mind of the eternal act of creation in the infinite I AM."[4] While the works of fancy are lifeless, mechanistic artifacts produced by the imposition of a predetermined form or by the operation of laws of association, the products of imagination display organic form, which, Coleridge says, "is innate. It shapes as it develops itself from within."[5] As Abrams remarks, however, "to substitute the concept of growth for the operation of a mechanism in the psychology of invention, seems merely to exchange one kind of determinism for another; while to replace the mental artisan-planner by the concept of organic self-generation makes it difficult, analogically, to justify the participation of consciousness in the creative process" (p. 173).

Organicist language was introduced in order to distinguish the servile and combinatory operations of fancy from the creativity and freedom of the imagination, but this representation of freedom ends by denying the freedom it was supposed to represent. Free will, conscious origination, becomes a crux in Coleridge, Abrams says, "because this runs counter to an inherent tendency of his elected analogue" (p. 174). The problem of the "elected analogue" illustrates the very issue that is at stake here: the freedom and power of the mind in relation to language. Coleridge's imagination imagined a new concept of imagination; he chose a new analogue in an act of freedom and

[4]S. T. Coleridge, *Biographia Literaria* (London: Dent, 1956), p. 167.
[5]Coleridge, *Shakespeare Criticism*, ed. T. M. Raysor (London: Constable, 1930), I, 223.

origination. But his elected analogue turned out, Abram says, to have an inherent tendency. It developed according to laws of its own, determined less by an act of origination than by an autonomous logic.

This organicist logic thus deconstructs itself, revealing the irresoluble paradox that is one of its greatest insights into the nature of language. The very figures that state the freedom and creativity of imagination and its products illustrate the limitations of that freedom which they were supposed to represent. More generally, one can say that no account of language can escape the aporia of structure and event. On the one hand, language seems the realm or medium in which consciousness can truly produce events, display its freedom in creative acts of origination. Language thus seems the realm of fresh starts and discontinuity. But, on the other hand, language is the realm of structures always already in place, as a plant is always already present in its prior state. Creative acts of imagination, like the sudden flowering of a plant, turn out to depend on and be limited by structures already in place; and linguistic creations, such as Coleridge's organic metaphors, function outside the control of an originating consciousness. Note that one cannot resolve this problem by seeking a compromise, in which linguistic structures are said to make possible a limited creativity and freedom—as if it were possible to divide language into what is free and what is determined. This is impossible, because the most common, banal, or resilient structures must have been produced, must once have been singular and creative events, while, on the other hand, the most radical creative acts turn out to be determined in various ways and to develop according to laws that are not the intentions of their "creators." In *The Mirror and the Lamp* this aporia is revealed in the attempt to make "organic" the name of both free origination and structural continuity.

This paradox or figure reproduces itself in surprising ways. Abrams argues, for example, that Coleridge's theory of mind—

his description of mind in terms of the organic processes of a living plant—"was, as he insisted, revolutionary; it was in fact part of a change in the habitual way of thinking, in all areas of intellectual enterprise, which is as sharp and dramatic as any the history of ideas can show" (p. 158). The description of mind as a plant, the representation of thought as a process of organic growth and continuity, is said to constitute a decisive rupture in the development of thought; and Coleridge's theory thus, by its very success, calls into question the appropriateness of characterizing thought as organic continuity and exfoliation.

Of course organicism is not merely a natural analogue. It is also a theological idea, one of the many modern critical concepts whose theological functions and origins *The Mirror and the Lamp* identifies. What is important here is not that individual concepts should have theological sources—that might be a matter of merely antiquarian interest—but that we are dealing with an economy, a system of terms based on the analogy, whether hidden or expressed, between the poet and God. "This analogy," Abrams writes, "opened the way for the introduction into criticism of a rich stock of linked ideas, accumulated over centuries of theological speculation" (p. 239). This "theocritical" system is what has made possible the wealth of critical speculation in our own day, and indeed, Abrams argues, holding up a mirror that shows us the self as other, if we fail to recognize to what extent the concepts and structures of literature and criticism are a displaced theology, "that is because we still live in what is essentially, although in derivative rather than direct manifestations, a Biblical culture, and readily mistake our hereditary ways of organizing experience for the conditions of reality and the universal forms of thought."[6]

Abrams discusses one particularly striking case in which critics

[6]M. H. Abrams, *Natural Supernaturalism* (London: Oxford University Press, 1971), pp. 65–66.

who thought they were challenging a Romantic and theological position were in fact simply occupying another position generated by the system of secularized theology, as if the system itself had determined in advance the possibilities of critical disagreement. This is the case of the poem as heterocosm:

> This parallel between God and the poet, and between God's relation to his world and the poet to his poem, fostered the earliest appearance of the doctrine, so widespread today, that a poem is a disguised self-revelation, in which its creator, "visibly-invisible," at the same time expresses and conceals himself. It turns out that the same parallel helped generate a conception of a work of art which seems equally modern, is hardly less widely current, and (having largely lost the marks of its origin) is often presented in explicit opposition to the cognate thesis that a poem is the expression of personality. This is the concept, at the heart of much of the "new criticism," that poetic statement and poetic truth are utterly diverse from scientific statement and scientific truth, in that a poem is an object-in-itself, a self-contained universe of discourse, of which we cannot demand that it be true to nature, but only, that it be true to itself. [P. 272]

One could argue, following Abrams' lead, that it was no accident that the New Criticism found itself implicated in a theological system; that indeed any criticism predicated upon the autonomy and teleological unity of the work will have a theological character.[7] What Abrams has done is to demonstrate the pervasiveness of what one might call the "theocritical system," which determines even opposing polemical positions; and he provides no expectation of escape from the logocentrism of this system.

But he does suggest that we can escape and indeed have escaped from the mimetic conception of mind and art: rejecting notions of the mind or work as mirror, we have, since the Romantic period, thought of the mind as lamp and the work as

---

[7]For an acute analysis of the theological nature of the freedom that is at stake in "purposive wholes without purpose," see Derrida, "Economimesis."

plant. And this shift from mirror to lamp is, he claims, part of "a change in the habitual way of thinking . . . as sharp and dramatic as any the history of ideas can show" (p. 158). If we are persuaded, as Abrams' readers usually are, that we have indeed made this decisive move from mirror to lamp, it is because we are convinced that *The Mirror and the Lamp* is an accurate mirror. It can convince us that this shift away from representation has taken place only by convincing us that it is accurately representing or reflecting what has taken place—accurately mirroring what is to be found in the texts. This persistence of mimesis, as the very ground of arguments that reject it, ought to arouse our suspicions that perhaps we have not left the order of mirrors and mirroring and that perhaps, on the contrary, lamps are only another version of mirrors and belong to the same system of specularity and representation.

Once these suspicions are aroused, a number of things confirm them. First, the notion of poem as heterocosm, which is supposed to have displaced the notion of the poem as imitation, is always justified by an appeal to mimeticism: the poet imitates the creative act of God or, at the very least, the generative activity of nature. The work can be a world in itself rather than an imitation of nature only if it is produced in a process that imitates the production of the world. Second, it could be argued that this notion of generative activity, supposed to be distinctive of lamps, is already implicit in conceptions of the mind as mirror. Here is Ernst Cassirer explicating the philosophy of the Enlightenment: "When the mind becomes a mirror of reality it is and remains a living mirror of the universe, and it is not simply the sum total of mere images but a whole composed of formative forces."[8] Here the mirror already has formative power; it is implicitly a lamp.

The difficulty of using the distinction between mirror and lamp for historical periodization is compounded when one looks

[8]Ernst Cassirer, *The Philosophy of the Enlightenment* (Boston: Beacon Press, 1966), p. 124.

JONATHAN CULLER

to Yeats, whose remarks in the introduction to the *Oxford Book of Modern Verse* provide the epigraph for *The Mirror and the Lamp:* "it must go further still; that soul must become its own betrayer, its own deliverer, the one activity, the mirror turn lamp."[9] What is this movement from mirror to lamp which Yeats, in 1936, says must go further still? It is the shift from Stendhal (who "described a masterpiece as a 'mirror dawdling down a lane'"), novelists "from Huysmans to Hemingway," Victorian poets, and modern poets who, Yeats says, feel they can "write a poem by recording the fortuitous scene or thought . . .—'I am sitting in a chair, there are three dead flies on a corner of the ceiling'"—a shift from these writers of the mirror to three Georgian poets: Walter James Turner, Herbert Read, and Dorothy Wellesley.[10] Though Yeats suggests, in remarks that he subsequently proposes to dismiss as "ancient history," that the Elizabethan and seventeenth-century poets and the Romantics can be classified with the Georgians, and the poets of the eighteenth century grouped with the Victorians and the moderns, this move alerts us to the fact that the distinction has, to say the least, a variable historical content and is primarily evaluative. (When poetry turns from lamp to mirror it loses, Yeats says, "bravado.") Since Abrams takes his epigraph from Yeats's discussion, one must at least consider the possibility that his separation of two historically distinct aesthetic theories may be a way of establishing an evaluative distinction, persuading us to prefer Romantic to eighteenth-century poetry by drawing upon the theological notions implicit in the Romantic description of the poet.

The mind or the poet as lamp: what is the force of that image? A lamp illuminates when it is dark, when there is not enough light to see. The light of a lamp stands in a determined relation to natural light, which it replaces or imitates. The meaning of *lamp* depends on this system, which makes it a substitute sun or

[9]W. B. Yeats, "Introduction," *Oxford Book of Modern Verse* (Oxford: Oxford University Press, 1936), p. xxxiii.
[10]Ibid., pp. xxvii–xxx.

source of light; its significance is established by a relation of mimesis. Doubtless there is a difference between the poet as lamp, projecting, by God's grace, a light like God's own, and the poet as mirror, reflecting the light provided by God; but both give us a system based on visibility, presence, and representation, where the mind or author casts light upon that which he perceives and represents. To put it bluntly, a mirror is no use without light, and there is no point in illuminating a scene unless something will register or reflect what is there. The economy of mimesis presupposes light; the lamp fits into that economy.

Abrams cites as an example of the romantic view the famous lines in which Coleridge, after hearing portions of *The Prelude,* speaks of its "theme hard as high!"

> of moments awful,
> Now in thy inner life, and now abroad,
> When power streamed from thee, and thy soul received
> A light reflected, as a light bestowed . . . [P. 60]

The passage seems to claim that Wordsworth thought he was a mirror when he was in fact a lamp, and it explains why it might be hard to tell the difference: in both cases light comes to one from nature, and the question is whether the light is bestowed by nature or whether nature is reflecting light that one originally cast in its direction. But wherever the light comes from, we have a system in which subject and object are present to one another in a light that makes possible a specular relationship, a relationship of correspondence: subject reflected in object and object in subject. The most compelling evidence for this view—that Romantic poetry of the lamp does not break with the economy of specularity but is part of it—comes from Abrams himself. When he identifies the exemplary Romantic project in *Natural Supernaturalism* he selects as "the manifesto of a central romantic enterprise" not a passage about lamps but the high argument of Wordsworth's preface to *The Excursion:*

JONATHAN CULLER

How exquisitely the individual Mind
. . . to the external World
Is fitted:—and how exquisitely, too,
Theme this but little heard of among Men,
The external world is fitted to the Mind.[11]

There is light here also (a good fitting requires light): light provided by the

dread Power,
Whose gracious favour is the primal source
Of all illumination.

This light makes possible the mirroring relationship, "fitting and
fitted," between subject and object. In showing the centrality of
this passage to the projects enunciated by Romantic theory,
Abrams has identified for us a mirror stage, in which the subject
grasps itself as object and attains self-awareness through this
specular fitting. Yeats, Abrams' expert on mirrors and lamps,
writes: "Mirror on mirror mirrored is all the show."[12]

"Mirror on mirror mirrored is all the show," I am suggesting,
when we are dealing with mirrors and lamps. It is the only show
on the mirror stage. But there are other shows on other stages,
and Abrams has given us a preview of some of them. Some of his
analyses are the beginnings of what one might call a deconstructive reading of Romantic theory: a reading attentive to its self-
deconstructive logic, to what exceeds the economy of mimesis
and specularity—such as plants that get out of hand and put in
question the power of origination that they were supposed to
represent. These analyses alert us to a tropology, a play of language that cannot be arrested by centering systems. Indeed,
Abrams' whole approach is predicated, as he tells us, upon the
insight that since critical terminology is borrowed and hence
figurative, the logic of the figures themselves will, to a consider-

[11]Abrams, *Natural Supernaturalism*, pp. 19–32.
[12]"The Statues," in *Collected Poems of W. B. Yeats* (New York: Macmillan, 1956),
p. 322.

able extent, determine critical thinking. A working out of that logic invariably reveals a certain excess, something that doesn't fit, is neither fitting nor fitted to the mirroring or specular relationship between subject and object.

The seductiveness of the mirror stage is its offer of totality and a vision of the self as a unified whole. What lies "beyond" the mirror stage is a loss of totality, the fragmentation of the body and the self—what Lacan calls the symbolic order. The child is born into the symbolic order in that he has a name that stands for him in the order of language, and because he already figures in an oedipal triangle that lies beyond the binary order of reflection. Though the child never leaves the mirror stage altogether —for he continues to identify with images of wholeness—he enters the symbolic order by accepting the fragmentation of the body (more specifically, in technical terms, castration) and by accepting the possibility that language brings of the discontinuity of the self.[13]

A reading of Romanticism attentive to what lies beyond the specularity of the mirror stage and the focus on correspondence between subject and object would follow two lines of inquiry. First, it would stress that even if poems are presented as specular encounters of mind and nature, they are intertextual constructs, revisionary responses to other texts, moments or fragments of a poetic process which, like the oedipal triangle, always precedes and exceeds the subject. Analysts working in this mode will be tempted to personalize the intertextual and reduce it to a specular struggle between a poet and a single great precursor, in whom he sees himself. This reduction can generate powerful readings but must appeal to a totalizing notion of the self which is irreparably subverted by aspects of language such readings must neglect: the uncertain status of citation and allusion, whose interpretation can never be limited by an authorial project, and the uncanny displacements of figural logic from one text to another.

[13]See Lacan, "Stade du miroir."

A second focus for a reading that sought to go beyond the mirror stage would be language itself, and in particular the written character which, for example, plays such strange roles in *The Prelude*. Language disrupts or displaces the self-sufficient visual presence of object to subject in the mirror stage. Poets may, of course, hope for a perfect correspondence between language and thought, knowing, as Wordsworth wrote, that "if words be not an incarnation of the thought but only a clothing for it, then surely they will prove an ill gift; such a one as those poisoned vestments, read of in the stories of superstitious times, which had power to consume and to alienate from his right mind the victim who put them on."[14] The child, told that in the language of adults he is "William" or "George" or "Mary," might well, if he could rise to philosophic complaint, find language an ill gift, garments he is loath to put on; but it is a gift he must accept—in the hope, as Wordsworth says, that it will become a sustaining yet invisible medium, like the air we breathe, or else a stable operative principle that can be taken for granted, like the force of gravity. "Language," Wordsworth continues after raising the specter of poisoned vestments, "Language, if it do not uphold and feed, and leave in quiet, like the power of gravitation or the air we breathe, is a counter-spirit, unremittingly and noiselessly at work to derange, to subvert, to lay waste, to vitiate, and to dissolve."

Today we are less sanguine than readers of Wordsworth have often been about the possibility that language might simply "leave in quiet." We are more inclined to subscribe to the doubts and uneasiness that Wordsworth here expresses with such power. (Indeed, with the current interest in the way the language of texts deranges, subverts, lays waste, vitiates, dissolves, and deconstructs, if one were to write *The Mirror and the Lamp* today one would have to give it a different title, such as, perhaps, *The Mire and the Swamp*.) But Abrams has already pointed the way to the mire, directing us in *The Mirror and the*

[14]Wordworth, "Essay on Epitaphs III," in *Wordsworth's Literary Criticism*, ed. W. J. B. Owen (London: Routledge, 1974). p. 154.

Lamp to Wordsworth's "Essay on Epitaphs," which, he says, "has not received adequate attention from students of Wordsworth's literary theory" (p. 111). When it does receive adequate attention—and this attention has begun with an excellent book by Frances Ferguson, *Wordsworth: Language as Counter-Spirit*—we may be able to answer such questions as why many of Wordsworth's most important statements on poetry come in comments on funerary inscriptions, the type of verse furthest removed from the specular relation between subject and object, and what we can learn about the function of "sincerity" in Wordsworth's theory from its prominence in this particular context, where ordinary notions of sincerity become problematic. This kind of inquiry would lead to an identification of what in Romantic theory and practice lies beyond the mirror stage.

It is rumored that one eminent critic, asked to read the manuscript of *The Mirror and the Lamp,* recommended publication but advised that the author cut out the discussion of mirrors and lamps and concentrate on doctrine. Fortunately the young author did not take this advice, and as a result he produced a book closely in touch with problems of literary language. Aware of the impossibility and undesirability of trying to reduce metaphors to a supposed literality, he pursues a logic of tropes that is unremittingly at work in our language and in the genealogy of our critical terms. He thus comes to figure in a tradition of writing that explores the peculiar logic of theoretical discourse and whose recent exponents include, for example, Jacques Derrida. *The Mirror and the Lamp* teaches us to explore systems of metaphor, and though the author would doubtless disown the work of those whose efforts continue his project of deconstructing the theological system of our critical thinking, the logic of his enterprise, like a plant, continues sending out roots, disseminating. We can therefore celebrate in *The Mirror and the Lamp* not only an achievement but also a future: a future whose ability to surprise and even to reverse previous conclusions is no small part of its power and interest.

A Reply

M. H. ABRAMS

A reply hardly seems appropriate to the occasion. I feel as
though I have been privileged to listen to orations at my own
funeral, and by the subject of such oratory the proper response
is a dead silence. As a professor standing before a captive audience, on the other hand, to maintain silence is patently not my
métier. So, in obedience to the behest of our chairman, I shall try
to recollect some thoughts that occurred to me in the course of
these last two days.

It's difficult to do so, because my senses are aswim with the
fragrance of the funeral bouquets that have been heaped upon
me. I have been called a mirror, a fountain, a lamp, and the
genie in the lamp; also an instrument, a sculptor, a creator, a
bottle opener, a master ophthalmologist, a Waring blender, a
spiral staircase, and a stage—according to Jonathan Culler, a
fixated mirror stage in an ongoing process, but according to
Wayne Booth, a moving mirror stage that keeps pace with the
history it reflects. More heady still were the bouquets in the
figure not of metaphor but of hyperbole. I've been compared,
with hints that it was not entirely to my disadvantage, with two
great historians of ideas and of critical theory whom I have
admiringly studied, A. O. Lovejoy and R. S. Crane, as well as
with such masters of literary and cultural history as Erich Auer-

bach, Ernst Curtius, and Ernst Cassirer. Then one of the eulogists mentioned Plato, and for a bewildering moment I almost expected ... Wayne Booth hailed me as a meta-metaphorist, or master critic, through diverse metaphoric perspectives, of humanity's grandest metaphoric visions. Larry Lipking claimed that, by Dr. Johnson's criterion of a century of continuing esteem, one of my books is already (give or take, of course, three-quarters of a century) a classic. And Tom McFarland, moving from natural to supernatural hyperbole, has nominated me a candidate for canonization—for admission, that is, to the enduring literary canon that is invulnerable to adverse criticism—conceding, however, that, though already beatified, I must await the final verdict of the synod qualified to administer the rites of passage.

With all due allowance for the epideictic figure of amplification, I confess that these flowers of rhetoric made me at first uneasy. But then, as I listened with a consciousness heightened by recent deconstructive hermeneutics, there dawned upon me the recognition that there was no need for concern—that if I didn't believe what the speakers said about me, the deep structure of their language revealed that they didn't either. All their ostensibly complimentary figures, when put to question, become problematic, and all the verbal bouquets they threw at me turn out to contain, if not brickbats, at least pebbles. One that gave me special pleasure, though its self-subversion was fairly close to the surface, was Wayne Booth's denominating me the doorkeeper of a house of ill repute who admits all comers; my delight was only slightly alloyed by his later qualification that the metaphor, though it conveyed some truth, fell short of the whole truth. Larry Lipking, proposing that my principal methods of proof are analogical and quasi-religious, compared my books to Bishop Butler's famous *Analogy of Religion*, even as he unwittingly provided clues that he doesn't believe, any more than I do, that Butler's elaborate arguments from analogy prove anything more than the resourcefulness of their proponent. By the immanent logic of his own figures, Tom McFarland's suggestion that I be canonized revealed itself in the sequel to be a covert proposal that I be embalmed and mummified, like a pharaoh in his desert tomb. And then there's McFarland's alternative comparison of my two long books to the twin towers of the World Trade Center, which dominate the skyline of Manhattan. One doesn't have to be a Freud, or a Lacan, to be suspicious of that figure of praise. I never approach New York without lamenting the intrusion upon its once exuberant skyline of Gothic and Art Deco spires by those two dour, dark, square-topped, overweening oblongs. No, Tom, it will do you no good to insist that you really think that the World Trade Center is beautiful, because it is to me a matter of certain knowledge that, in the depths of your unconscious, your aesthetic judgments are no less infallible than my own.

In thus dwelling on metaphors and on what they say—and what they can be hermeneutically teased into really saying—I am following the lead of several of the speakers on this occasion, whose commentaries, and even titles, show their preoccupation with a single aspect of my writings; that is, my use of changes in radical, constitutive metaphors as one key to important shifts in the intellectual and cultural history of the West. In this preoccupation, our speakers are attuned to what Romantic writers called "the spirit of the age." For the linguistic turn common to philosophy, literary criticism, and the human sciences during the last half-century has, in the last five years or so, tended to focus on the role of metaphor in speech and writing. An incidental result, to judge by what our speakers said, has been to precipitate my earlier discussions of thought-constitutive metaphors out of their placid backwater into the mainstream of present semiotic concern.

Or more than into the mainstream, according to Jonathan Culler—into the radical forefront; for it is Culler's contention that my writings are an early instance, at the very least a "preview," of the deconstructive reading of the play of figurative economies in a text, of which Jacques Derrida is the major exponent. This claim evoked in me what Wordsworth called a shock of mild surprise, and an initial skepticism. But as Larry Lipking has remarked, Culler, in addition to being brilliant, is plausible. He went on to point out that in expounding the role of radical metaphors in the philosophies of mind, art, and history, I had shown that all representations of these matters are willy-nilly metaphorical; that many of these radical metaphors are theotropic, in that they can be traced to a theological provenience; and that any one metaphor both entails and turns into its seeming opposite, which in turn entails its progenitive opponent. Culler then adduced, from my narrative of evolving metaphors, dramatic instances in which, as he put it, a radical metaphor implicates an unwitting and unwanted "aporia" which subverts the ground of the discoveries that the metaphor makes possible. Looking back from the vantage point that Culler so acutely provides, I am compelled to agree that I can indeed be plausibly represented as a precursor of the disseminating strategies of Jacques Derrida; who, it seems safe to say, has never read a word that I have written.

I agree, that is (as Culler is aware), within limits. To indicate what some of those limits are, let's take Culler's first citation, a passage from *The Mirror and the Lamp* which Tom McFarland had earlier alluded to for another purpose. There I said, in a comment on Coleridge's critical organicism, "Only let the vehicles of his metaphors come alive, and you see all the objects of criticism writhe surrealistically into plants or parts of plants, growing in tropical profusion." Culler discriminates in my own mildly ironic comment on Coleridge's plant figures a doubly punning figuration: "Planted in Abrams' lively language is . . . a tropism, a tropical profusion: the pun on tropes and tropics might even count as mild 'surrealistic writhing.' "

Neither when I wrote that passage nor at any time afterward was I aware of these puns. Yet I must admit, now that Culler has brought them to my attention, that they are patently in my text.

The question arises: Who made those puns? When I wrote the text, I was competent enough in the use of the adjective "tropical" to know that it could be applied both geographically, to the Torrid Zone, and rhetorically, to a linguistic "turn" or figure of speech. I had also read the Mock Turtle's delightful summary of the elementary-school curriculum, which I recollect (not, I think, entirely accurately) as "reeling, writhing, and the branches of arithmetic, including long and short derision." Since I possessed this background information, should I be said to have made those puns, but by an intention below the level of consciousness? My own conclusion is that, given the implicit criteria according to which we make such linguistic attributions, this is a borderline case. I have grounds, but not decisive ones, for asserting that I made those puns, although unwittingly. I also have grounds, equally inconclusive, for asserting that not I but Jonathan Culler made those puns, on the occasion of some phrases I innocently wrote. Or else I can choose to assert that such a borderline case is not strictly decidable, and may be left undecided between me and Culler.

What Culler himself proposes, however, is a third alternative: that neither I nor he made those puns, but that language itself made them. For my text is evidence that "language can lead a life of its own, even run wild," because "unable to control its own tropology." And in claiming that what I said about Coleridge's metaphors can be accounted "the beginning" of a "deconstructive reading"—"the revelation of a self-deconstructive movement within romantic discourse, whose major insights are aporias"—Culler also suggests that, by the secret compulsion of its inner logic, my own language reveals its self-deconstructive workings in the very sentences in which I expound my incipiently deconstructive reading of Coleridge; especially, one may perhaps presume, in the unwitting aporia by which my language reveals itself to be not speech, but a mode of writing/writhing.

One recognizes in Culler's account the basic presumption both of structuralist and deconstructuralist procedures, which is often expressed by quoting Heidegger, "Die Sprache spricht, nicht der Mensch"—with the proviso, of course, that language always speaks in accordance with a special interpretation of the theory of Ferdinand de Saussure. Now, the assertion that man doesn't speak, that only language speaks, has a strong melodramatic pathos, and its structuralist applications have led to interesting insights into the degree to which, when we use language, language is also using us. But this assertion is figurative, and Coleridge, himself a master metaphorist, long ago warned us (a warning I quoted early in *The Mirror and the Lamp*) that "no simile runs on all four legs." Or as Culler, echoing Derrida, put the matter, the logic of figurative language "invariably reveals a certain excess: something that doesn't fit." It seems to me that French theorists, overlooking their own caveats, have evolved from Heidegger's principle the view, not only that we human beings don't speak, but that we don't operationally exist—that "the author is dead" and the human reader liquidated in the sea of linguicity; that man himself is no more than "a simple fold in our language" that is fated to disappear; hence that deconstructive interpretation, as Derrida puts it, must try "to pass beyond man and humanism." In Culler's excellent expositions and applications of structuralist and poststructuralist theory, he usually qualifies the characteristic extremes of Gallic rationalism by an admixture of Anglo-Saxon common sense and caution; yet in his talk here, he indicated his acquiescence to the extreme view when he displaced the author as an "originating consciousness" by the deconstructive play of a language that is compelled by an inner entelechy, its "autonomous logic."

Well, that marks one limit to Culler's representation of my work as figuring in a tradition that leads to Derrida: I believe that we can neither understand language nor analyze its workings with any adequacy except by assigning indispensable functions to human beings, minds, and initiatives. To take a recent instance: a few years ago Derrida published in *Glyph* an earlier talk in which he included a respectful critique of John

Austin's theory of illocutionary acts, and especially of Austin's view that such acts often have a decidable meaning and Austin's alleged assumption that linguistic communication involves a conscious subject who is fully aware of his intended meaning. To this the philosopher John Searle wrote a curt and rather contemptuous reply, asserting not only that Derrida had misunderstood Austin, but that his commentary is often confused and reveals a failure to grasp basic concepts concerning the use of language in speech and writing. To this reply Derrida in turn replied, at great length. Among other things, he deconstructed Searle into "three + *n* authors" and reconstituted this multiple into a corporation he called "Sarl" (the standard abbreviation for *Societé à responsabilité limitée*), and cited almost the whole of Sarl's reply within a dialectic designed to show that where Sarl wasn't dead wrong, or perhaps deliberately falsifying, he was bringing objections against Derrida's claims which in fact were assertions plagiarized from Derrida's essay itself. The hermeneutic magician, by an ultimate feat of thaumaturgy, then made himself disappear, deconstructing himself into a printed signature, "Jacques Derrida," which he represented as undecidable in its authenticity, provenience, reference, and material location. Dazzled though I am by this display, I remain unconvinced that there is nothing more than a reduplicable printed signature at each end of this linguistic transaction of reply and counterreply. At the latter end of the transaction, for example, it was not simply language that—with no show of hesitation, incidentally, about the decidability of Searle's negative arguments and sentiments—was nettled into producing ninety-three pages of counterarguments, *ad hominem* demolition, caustic ironies, and magisterial reprimand. As I read it, the language merely manifests that *someone* was nettled, and I am persuaded, despite the legerdemain with the printed signature, that the someone was none other than a human being named Jacques Derrida.

There is another important boundary to Culler's equation between my way of dealing with metaphors in intellectual discourse and the procedures of poststructuralists. As Culler represents these procedures, not only is the play of metaphors determined by the immanent logic of language, but the play takes place without any possibility of reference beyond the limits of language itself. There is, in Derrida's formulation of this view, no "outside of language" to which the metaphors apply, for when we undertake to say what they signify, we have no resort except to elucidate words and metaphors by a chain of substitute words and metaphors, and so on without end. It is significant, however, that among the countless metaphors that have been used during the long history of intellection in the West, a select number exhibit a powerful survival value. To borrow a useful formulation from Tom McFarland's account of the making of a literary classic, we find a canon formation in the history of constitutive metaphors. In discussions of works of art, for example, such metaphors as the mirror, the growing plant, the artist as creator, and his work as a heterocosm or second world survive and proliferate, while other metaphors simply come and go. As an example: Roland Barthes recently published a book that applied to literary texts an almost unprecedented set of interrelated metaphors. Susan Sontag had written an essay, "Against Interpretation," which concluded with the plea that "in place of a hermeneutics we need an erotics of art." In a sustained display of witty ingenuity, Barthes exploited the analogy between reading a literary text and, not love, but making love: a text that is readily *lisible* according to conventional literary codes yields at most *plaisir;* it is only in reading a text that radically violates these codes that you explode into *jouissance,* orgasmic ecstasy. These new critical metaphors have their attractions, but I think it safe to predict that they won't achieve the canonical status of other metaphors such as mirrors, plants, creators, and heterocosms.

How are we to account for the survival and canonical status of these and other metaphors in the criticism of art? I don't think we can find the answer by reference to the mysterious goings-on of the logic of language, but only by reference to something beyond language which, applying loose-boundaried criteria, we identify as works of art. Historically, each of these metaphors has demonstrated its ability to clarify, refine, and organize our knowledge of these works of art; but history also has demonstrated that none of these metaphors is in itself coincident with, or adequate to, the phenomena to which it is applied. In various writings I have undertaken to show how, in the course of time, a new metaphor arises which demonstrates its revelatory power at the same time that it reveals the inadequacies of preceding metaphors, is exploited until it becomes the predominant metaphor of an era, and is in turn displaced from its central position, yet—and this is an aspect inadequately heeded by some of the commentators on my work in this symposium—keeps recurring persistently in later eras. Such a canonical metaphor, in my view, flourishes and recurs because its particular pertinence and area of focus make it profitable in critical discourse. And it is profitable because, even though less than fully adequate, it provides us with a fuller understanding of something beyond its own internal economy.

Well, that marks the second limit to the coincidence that Culler has asserted between my treatment of metaphors and their treatment in poststructuralist writings. I believe not only that interpretation involves human beings at each end of a language transaction, whether spoken or written, but also that language can signify, and so bring to our attention, aspects of things that exist outside of language, even when those things are works of literature which themselves consist of a signifying language.

While I listened to our various speakers on the subject of metaphor, a notion occurred to me which I will hazard formulating by way of conclusion. The grand constitutive metaphors by which we have tried to make sense of ourselves and our doings are perforce taken from either natural or artificial objects and processes. What these metaphors are applied to, on the other hand, are human thought, speech, interpretation, actions, and makings. These latter involve elemental aspects we identify by such terms as consciousness, intention, purpose, design. I know that these terms can all, by reference to an etymological dictionary, be shown to be themselves adequated metaphors, therefore seemingly derivative, and eligible for deconstruction by Derrida and others into pseudo-references to presences that deliquesce into absences. My own claim, however, is that such terms, however derived linguistically, signify matters that are elementary and irreducible in that they are *systematically* primitive, in any language competent to approximate an adequate understanding of what human beings say, do, and make, whether in art or the sciences or *les sciences humaines*.

The human compulsion not only to say, do, and make but also to understand what we say, do, and make enforces a discourse about these processes and products of consciousness, intention, purpose, and design. This discourse unavoidably involves metaphors whose vehicles are natural or artificial objects, and since none of these objects runs on all fours with the human primitives it undertakes to define and take into account, each metaphor, however pertinent, remains inadequate. It is because a number of metaphoric vehicles are pertinent, yet no one is adequate, that the history I undertook to narrate displays the recurrent emergence, exploitation, displacement, and supplementation of constitutive metaphors; this historical process seems to me to be, in the long run, profitable to understanding, in that it provides (as Wayne Booth quoted my saying) a vision in depth in place of a two-dimensional view of the complex realities with which the metaphors engage. Culler's alternative account of this history—by assigning all initiative and motion to an entelechy determining the working of language from within, instead of to human purposes and the human desire to understand—interprets the shifts from metaphor to metaphor not as supplementary or complementary, but as the manifestation of an aporia, or inner contradiction, which remorselessly compels all discourse, as he says, to self-deconstruction, vitiation, subversion, and dissolution. But I believe that my account, by systematically absolving certain human primitives from dissolution, is the only one that provides something like an adequate understanding in place of a radical, annihilating skepticism with respect to matters of deep human concern. So, if I were to rewrite my first book about constitutive metaphors today, I would call it still *The Mirror and the Lamp* and not, as Culler suggests I might call it, *The Mire and the Swamp*.

What I have said does not constitute a knockout argument, far less the demonstration of an absolute foundation, for my standpoint. I believe, in fact, that this matter of the choice of the primitives for intellectual discourse is beyond all demonstrative argument except—and the exception is of high consequence—the pragmatic argument of the profitability for our understanding in choosing one set of intellectual premises over another. What I have said, then, is really an announcement of where I take my stand—a stand on certain primitives to be used in our explanative discourse about human talking, doing, and making. Which amounts to the confession that, despite immersion in the deconstructive element of our time, I remain an unreconstructed humanist.

Let me take this opportunity warmly to thank all of these speakers. They are the best group of critics I've ever had the pleasure of listening to on a single occasion. I trust it will not be taken as ingratitude or recalcitrance, but only as symptomatic of the nature of humanistic dialogue, if I admit that I agree only in part with what any of them has said that I've said, and much less with what any of them has said about me. But I recognize that, in the latter instance, they were operating within the constraints of a double decorum: what it is appropriate to say on this ritual occasion, and what it is appropriate to say in public about a friend. Because all these speakers are old friends of mine, and some of them former students. They were very kind to come and very generous (as I've learned from the organizers of these academic obsequies) to volunteer their services.

A Reply

Yes, I did say "services," and your laughter shows me that I have uttered a pun, though one I had no intention of uttering. Who made that pun? The premises of deconstructive interpretation give me the option of attributing the pun to the inner intentionality of language itself. But I am a humanist, so I hereby assume full credit for having inadvertently made a very bad pun.

A Bibliography of M. H. Abrams

STUART A. ENDE

When M. H. Abrams used to teach the sophomore survey course for English majors at Cornell, a handout cautioned eager writers: "It is unnecessary to compliment the genius of famous men." The bibliography that follows perhaps evades this stricture, for though it is certainly a compliment, it is so by implication: the works of Professor Abrams can be found in homes and libraries from Japan to Romania; this list gives some idea of the scope of the work. It could not have been compiled without the help of my very able research assistant, Carol Pearson. After our list was finished it was sent to Professor Abrams for corroboration and additions. It is therefore as complete as we were able to make it and, we hope, serviceable.

Books

1. *The Milk of Paradise: The Effect of Opium Visions on the Works of De Quincey, Crabbe, Francis Thompson, and Coleridge.* Cambridge, Mass.: Harvard University Press, 1934. Half-title: Harvard Honors Theses in English, no. 7. "300 copies of this book have been printed and the type distributed."
   Reprinted by Folcroft Press, Folcroft, Pa., 1969; Harper & Row, New York, 1970 (Perennial Library); Octagon Books, New York, 1971 (this edition includes as an appendix George Crabbe's *The World of Dreams* and *Sir Eustace Grey* and Francis Thompson's *Finis Coronat Opus*).

2. "The Mirror and the Lamp: A Study of the Transition to Romantic Theories of Poetry and Criticism." Ph.D. thesis, Harvard University, 1940. Typewritten. 2 vols.

3. *The Mirror and the Lamp: Romantic Theory and the Critical Tradition.* New York: Oxford University Press, 1953.

> Reprinted by W. W. Norton, New York, 1958 (The Norton Library, N502); Oxford University Press, London and New York, 1960 and 1971 (A Galaxy Book, GB 360).
> Also translated into Spanish, German, Italian, Romanian, Japanese.
> Winner of the Christian Gauss Prize, 1954.

4. *A Glossary of Literary Terms.* Based on the original version by Dan S. Norton and Peters Rushton. New York: Rinehart, 1957. (The Rinehart English Pamphlet Series.)

> 2d ed., 1965.
> 3d ed., New York, 1971; Bangkok, Thailand, 1975.

5. *Natural Supernaturalism: Tradition and Revolution in Romantic Literature.* New York: W. W. Norton, 1971.

> Reprinted by W. W. Norton, New York, 1973 (The Norton Library).
> Winner of the James Russell Lowell Prize, 1972.

Books Edited

6. *The Poetry of Pope: A Selection.* New York: Appleton-Century-Crofts, 1954 (Crofts Classics).

7. *Literature and Belief* (with an Introduction). New York: Columbia University Press, 1958 (English Institute Essays, 1957).

8. *English Romantic Poets: Modern Essays in Criticism.* New York: Oxford University Press, 1960 (A Galaxy Book, GB 35).

> 2d ed., 1975.

9. General ed., with others. *The Norton Anthology of English Literature.* 2 vols. New York: W. W. Norton, 1962.

> 2d ed., 1968.
> 3d ed., 1974.
> 4th ed., 1979.
> General ed., with others. *The Norton Anthology of English Literature.* Major authors edition. New York: W. W. Norton, 1962.
> 2d ed., 1968.
> 3d ed., 1975.

10. *Wordsworth: A Collection of Critical Essays.* Twentieth Century Views series. Englewood Cliffs, N.J.: Prentice-Hall, 1972.

11. With Jonathan Wordsworth and Stephen Gill. *William Wordsworth: The Prelude: 1799, 1805, 1850.* New York and London: W. W. Norton, 1979.

Contributions to Books

12. "Wordsworth and Coleridge on Diction and Figures." In *English Institute Essays: 1952,* ed. Alan S. Downer (New York: Columbia University Press, 1954), pp. 171–201.
    Reprinted in abridged form in *Coleridge: A Collection of Critical Essays,* ed. Kathleen Coburn (Englewood Cliffs, N.J.: Prentice-Hall, 1967), pp. 125–36.
13. "Belief and the Suspension of Disbelief." In *Literature and Belief,* ed. with an Introduction by M. H. Abrams, pp. 1–30.
    Reprinted in *Literary Criticism, Idea and Act: The English Institute, 1939–1972: Selected Essays,* ed. William K. Wimsatt (Berkeley: University of California Press, 1974), pp. 149–69.
14. "Dr. Johnson's Spectacles." In *New Light on Dr. Johnson: Essays on the Occasion of His 250th Birthday,* ed. Frederick W. Hilles (New Haven: Yale University Press, 1959), pp. 177–87.
15. "Five Types of *Lycidas.*" In *Lycidas: The Tradition and the Poem,* ed. C. A. Patrides, Foreword by M. H. Abrams (New York: Holt, Rinehart & Winston, 1961), pp. 212–31.
    Reprinted as "Five Ways of Reading 'Lycidas,'" in *Varieties of Literary Experience: Eighteen Essays in World Literature,* ed. Stanley B. Burnshaw (New York: New York University Press, 1962), pp. 1–29.
16. "English Romanticism: The Spirit of the Age." In *Romanticism Reconsidered: Selected Papers from the English Institute* (English Institute Essays, 1962), ed. Northrop Frye (New York and London: Columbia University Press, 1963), pp. 26–72.
    Reprinted in *Romanticism and Consciousness,* ed. Harold Bloom (New York: W. W. Norton, 1970), pp. 90–119.
    Reprinted in *Romanticism: Points of View,* ed. R. F. Gleckner and G. E. Enscoe, 2d ed. (Englewood Cliffs, N.J.: Prentice-Hall, 1970), pp. 314–30.
17. "Newton's Rainbow and the Poet's." Reprinted from *The Mirror and the Lamp* in *Modern Criticism: Theory and Practice,* ed. Walter Sutton and Richard Foster (New York: Odyssey Press. 1963), pp. 367–73.
18. "Structure and Style in the Greater Romantic Lyric." In *From Sensibility to Romanticism: Essays Presented to Frederick A. Pottle,* ed. Frederick W. Hilles and Harold Bloom (New York: Oxford University Press, 1965), pp. 527–60.

[179]

Reprinted in *Romanticism and Consciousness*, ed. Harold Bloom (New York: W. W. Norton, 1970), pp. 201-29.

19. "Theories of Poetry." In *Princeton Encyclopedia of Poetry and Poetics*, ed. Alex Preminger and others (Princeton: Princeton University Press, 1965), pp. 639-49.

20. "Orientation of Critical Theories." Reprinted from *The Mirror and the Lamp* in *The Practice of Criticism*, ed. Sheldon P. Zitner, James D. Kissane, and M. M. Liberman (Glenview, Ill.: Scott, Foresman, 1966).

21. "Coleridge, Baudelaire, and Modernist Poetics." In *Immanente Aesthetik, Aesthetische Reflexion: Lyrik als Paradigma der Moderne*, ed. W. Iser (Munich, 1966), pp. 113-38.

22. "Mechanical and Organic Psychologies of Literary Invention." In *English Literature and British Philosophy: A Collection of Essays*, ed. S. P. Rosenbaum (Chicago and London: University of Chicago Press, 1971), pp. 136-67.

23. "Orientation of Critical Theories." Reprinted from *The Mirror and the Lamp* in *Twentieth-Century Literary Criticism*, ed. David Lodge (London: Longman, 1972), pp. 1-26.

24. "Two Roads to Wordsworth." In *Wordsworth: A Collection of Critical Essays*. Twentieth Century Views series. (Englewood Cliffs, N.J.: Prentice-Hall, 1972), pp. 1-11.

25. "What's the Use of Theorizing about the Arts?" In *In Search of Literary Theory*, ed. Morton W. Bloomfield (Ithaca: Cornell University Press, 1972), pp. 1-54.

26. "Coleridge and the Romantic Vision of the World." In *Coleridge's Variety: Bicentenary Studies*, ed. John Beer (Pittsburgh: University of Pittsburgh Press, 1974), pp. 101-33, 248-49.

27. "The Language and Methods of Humanism." In *The Philosophy of the Curriculum: The Need for General Education*, ed. Sidney Hook, Paul Kurtz, and Miro Todorovich (Buffalo: Prometheus Books, 1975), pp. 89-97.

Contributions to Periodicals

28. "Unconscious Expectations in the Reading of Poetry." *English Literary History*, 9 (December 1942), 235-44. An early version of "Dr. Johnson's Spectacles" (item 14 above).

29. "Archetypal Analogies in the Language of Criticism." *University of Toronto Quarterly*, 18 (July 1949), 313-27.

30. "The Correspondent Breeze: A Romantic Metaphor." *Kenyon Re-*

A Bibliography of M. H. Abrams

view, 19 (Winter 1957), 113–30. A revised version of this article is included in *English Romantic Poets: Modern Essays in Criticism* (item 8 above).

31. "Belief and Disbelief." *University of Toronto Quarterly*, 27 (January 1958), 117–36.
32. "Coleridge's 'A Light in Sound': Science, Metascience, and Poetic Imagination." *Proceedings of the American Philosophical Society*, 116 (December 1972), 458–76.
33. "Morse Peckham's 'Romanticism and Behavior': A Reply." *Philosophic Exchange: The Annual Proceedings of the Center for Philosophic Exchange*, 1 (Summer 1974), 85–92.
34. "A Note on Wittgenstein and Literary Criticism." *English Literary History*, 41 (Winter 1974), 541–54.
35. "Rationality and Imagination in Cultural History: A Reply to Wayne Booth." *Critical Inquiry*, 2 (Spring 1976), 447–64.
36. "The Deconstructive Angel." *Critical Inquiry*, 3 (Spring 1977), 425–38.
37. "Behaviorism and Deconstruction: A Comment on Morse Peckham's 'The Infinitude of Pluralism.'" *Critical Inquiry*, 4 (Autumn 1977), 181–93.
38. "How to Do Things with Texts." *Partisan Review*, 46 (October 1979), 566–88.

Reviews

39. Review, Joseph Warren Beach, *A Romantic View of Poetry*. *Modern Language Notes*, 60 (June 1945), 427–28.
40. Review, *The Philosophical Lectures of Samuel Taylor Coleridge*, ed. Kathleen Coburn. *University of Toronto Quarterly*, 20 (January 1951), 206–9.
41. Review, *The Portable Coleridge*, ed. Ivor Armstrong Richards. *Furioso*, Spring 1951, 75–79.
42. "The Truth about Dr. Johnson." Review, Jean H. Hagstrum, *Samuel Johnson's Literary Criticism*. *Kenyon Review*, 16 (Spring 1954), 307–13.
43. Review, Herbert Read, *The True Voice of Feeling: Studies in English Romantic Poetry*. *Modern Philology*, 52 (August 1954), 67–69.
44. "The Newer Criticism: Prisoner of Logical Positivism?" Review, Philip Wheelwright, *The Burning Fountain: A Study in the Language of Symbolism*. *Kenyon Review*, 17 (Winter 1955), 139–43.
45. "The Course of Criticism." Review, René Wellek, *A History of*

STUART A. ENDE

Modern Criticism: 1750–1830, vols. 1 and 2. *Yale Review*, 45 (Autumn 1955), 146–49.

46. Review, Elisabeth Schneider, *Coleridge, Opium and "Kubla Khan."* *Modern Language Notes*, 70 (March 1955), 216–19.

47. Joint review, *Coleridge on the Seventeenth Century*, ed. Roberta Florence Brinkley, and George Whalley, *Coleridge and Sara Hutchinson, and the Asra Poems. Modern Language Notes*, 72 (January 1957), 56–60.

48. "Professional Aesthetics." Review, Milton C. Nahm, *The Artist as Creator. Kenyon Review*, 19 (Spring 1957), 302–6.

49. Review, Frank Kermode, *Romantic Image. Victorian Studies*, 2 (September 1958), 75–77.

50. Review, *The Critical Works of Thomas Rymer*, ed. Curt A. Zimansky. *Modern Philology*, 55 (February 1958), 206–8.

51. Review, James Volant Baker, *The Sacred River: Coleridge's Theory of the Imagination. Modern Philology*, 56 (November 1958), 139–41.

52. Review, Isabel Hungerland, *Poetic Discourse. Philosophical Review*, 78 (July 1959), 411–13.

53. Review, Northrop Frye, *Anatomy of Criticism. University of Toronto Quarterly*, 28 (January 1959), 190–96.

54. Review, Ernest Lee Tuveson, *The Imagination as a Means of Grace: Locke and the Aesthetics of Romanticism. Modern Language Notes*, 78 (December 1961), 880–85.

55. Review, Owen Barfield, *What Coleridge Thought. Ohio Review*, 13 (Spring 1972), 84–89.

[1 8 2]

High Romantic Argument

Designed by Richard E. Rosenbaum.
Composed by The Composing Room of Michigan, Inc.
in 10 point Baskerville V.I.P., 3 points leaded,
with display lines in Baskerville.
Printed offset by Thomson/Shore, Inc. on
Warren's Olde Style Wove, 60 pound basis.
Bound by John H. Dekker & Sons, Inc.
in Joanna book cloth.